The
Function
of
Bibliography

by the same author

Bibliographical Control and Service

The
Function
of
Bibliography

by
Roy Stokes

A Grafton Book

André Deutsch

FIRST PUBLISHED 1969 BY
ANDRE DEUTSCH LIMITED
105 GREAT RUSSELL STREET
LONDON WC1
COPYRIGHT © 1969 BY ROY STOKES
ALL RIGHTS RESERVED
PRINTED IN GREAT BRITAIN BY
EBENEZER BAYLIS & SON LTD
THE TRINITY PRESS
WORCESTER AND LONDON

SBN 233 96012 0

Acknowledgements

Over the years during which I have been teaching bibliography, the problems surrounding its definition and function have been constantly under review. My first thanks must, as always, be extended to the students, and especially those of the Loughborough School of Librarianship, with whom these questions have been discussed. My thanks go also to the students in my bibliography classes in the United States, in the Schools of Librarianship in the University of California (Los Angeles); Simmons College, Boston; and most recently those of the Graduate School during my year at the University of Pittsburgh. The year in Pittsburgh also brought the opportunity to use the collections in the Hunt Botanical Library in the Carnegie University of Technology and, above all, to appreciate the superlative bibliographical work in its catalogue to which much reference is made.

It is difficult to write on any aspect of bibliography without a consciousness of the debt to the bibliographers of the past and, in particular to the great triumvirate of Pollard, McKerrow and Greg. Their influence will continue to be felt for generations yet to come. Much of their work was done under the general auspices of the Bibliographical Society and I am grateful to the Council of the Bibliographical Society for permission to quote from the publications of the Society and particularly from the contributions of Pollard and Greg to the *Transactions* of the Society. Many potent forces are still at work in bibliographical studies and the words and ideas of several living bibliographers will equally be found in these pages. I owe an especial debt of gratitude to Professor Fredson Bowers of the University of Virginia for allowing me to quote from several of his writings.

Contents

Introduction

Anyone who is working in any field of bibliography soon becomes accustomed to the question, 'What *is* bibliography?' The standard answers to this are inclined to leave as many problems behind them as they satisfy because the question must generally be interpreted in the light of the practitioner's own personal interests. In an age of increasing specialization bibliography has reaped all the advantages and disadvantages which are consequent upon this development. The past fifty years have seen notable progress in bibliographical studies and the field, which a century ago could be comprehended by one man, now nurtures hundreds of specialists. The strides which have been made have revolutionized the whole of bibliography and many of its specialized aspects have reached a degree of sophistication and maturity which could not have been envisaged only a short time ago. This has been, and continues to be, to the general good but there is a darker side to the moon as well.

We have witnessed a half century in which specialists can no longer talk with real understanding to other specialists in what is broadly the same field of study. The details are splendid but the picture as a whole loses a lot of its impact. So soon as any field of study loses contact with related studies and attempts to exist in isolation it begins to lose its effectiveness. Something then needs to be done to bind up the parts and create a mutual awareness of interdependency. The chapters which follow are an essay along these lines.

A definition, even a good definition, can produce a picture of the original without it's ever really becoming alive. An orange and a spiral staircase have for generations been posed as problems of this kind. The only valid definition of an orange is to eat one or of a spiral staircase to climb one. Or, as a children's book has put it with commendable clarity, 'A hole is to dig.' Because of this the chapters here on the various aspects of bibliography 'define' their subjects in different ways. In the main I have attempted to indicate the function of bibliography through the activities, the problems, the utility and the practice of the constituent parts.

As each segment of the whole takes on some definite form and substance it will be easier to appreciate not only the role of each part but also the inter-relationships of them all. It is a very opportune moment to reflect upon the mutual aid which should exist among bibliographical studies, because this has not always been apparent in recent years. They are, as A. W. Pollard said, all studies under *the big umbrella*.

I

The definition of bibliography

No initial difficulty in approaching the study of bibliography is greater than the understanding of precisely what is meant by the word. A basic confusion is rooted in the fact that it is a term of which one very common meaning has tended to overshadow all others. In the majority of cases the word is used to convey the simple idea of 'a list of books'. Even in this most limited of all connotations it is more usual to mis-apply the word to cover any such listing of books, irrespective of selectivity or comprehensiveness, than to employ it with its full bibliographical significance.

To the average layman, if indeed he is conscious of the word at all, this is all that is implied by bibliography and a bibliographer is nothing more than the individual who compiles such a list. The bibliographer can expect to assume all the benign indignity which was showered upon the lexicographer with Johnson's definition of 'a harmless drudge'. Any correction of this general impression would now, after many years of regular usage, be difficult; especially so since the meaning is not so much incorrect as partial.

It has frequently been pointed out that the word itself is unfortunate since, etymologically, it means the *writing* of books. This is the first meaning given to the word in the *Oxford English Dictionary*, but there designated as obsolete. This same source gives as the earliest use in this sense the entry in J. Phillipps' *The New World of English Words* in 1678 (Wing P. 2072).

The word 'bibliographer' as distinct from bibliography is earlier and was recorded in 1656 by Thomas Blount (second edition of his *The Academic of Eloquence* Wing B. 3322) with the meaning 'writer of books; Scrivener'. The use of the word in this specialized sense of a scrivener was of limited duration. Its last usage was traced by A. W. Pollard to 1761.[1] In Fenning's *English Dictionary* of that year, a bibliographer was described as 'one who writes or copies books'. Apart from this period from the mid-seventeenth to the mid-eighteenth centuries, during which this usage was in some currency, it is unlikely that it will ever be encountered to any great extent. It is, indeed, difficult to imagine that its use could ever have been considerable in either Blount's or Phillipps' time since much longer established words were already current. Throughout the whole of the manuscript period, during which books were being extensively written, in a non-authorial sense, or copied, the terms 'copyist' or 'scrivener', seem to have sufficed. It is difficult to see exactly why this particular usage of 'bibliography' and 'bibliographer' should have arisen at this particular time. The reason for its cessation in use is more understandable. Pollard believed that it was in France in the eighteenth century that the change was accomplished from the meaning of 'a writing of books' to 'a writing about books'. This was perfectly consistent with the increase in that kind of writing, chiefly under the stimulus of the new wave of book collecting, especially in France. DeBure's *Bibliographie Instructive* of 1763 stands as a witness of this new style of writing and this changing sense of the word.

This usage gained somewhat more formal support decades later when Peignot defined a bibliographer as one who made a special study of the knowledge of books, of literary history, and of all that related to the art of printing.[2] The new meaning gained acceptance in England in the writings of Thomas Frognall Dibdin early in the nineteenth century and met with

---

[1] *Encyclopaedia Britannica.* 11th edition. 1911. Vol. 3. p. 908

[2] *PEIGNOT*, Etienne Gabriel, *Dictionnaire Raisonné de Bibliologie.* 3 vols. Paris. 1802–4.

considerable approval among other writers. There was some rivalry to the word. Robert Southey preferred 'bibliology' but received very little general support, although the term 'book-lore' has occasionally been met in an attempt to shift the emphasis in the same direction. If support for Southey's usage has been limited on a strictly statistical count, it can, neverthe-less, claim to have had some authoritative support. When A. W. Pollard wrote the article on the subject for the eleventh edi-tion of the *Encyclopaedia Britannica*, he headed it 'Bibliography and bibliology'. On two separate occasions, in addresses to the Bibliographical Society in 1912 and 1932, Sir Walter Greg also half regretted 'that "bibliology" is past praying for' since it de-fined the study more precisely than the accepted word. Such championship cannot be lightly set aside, nevertheless it is now quite certain that 'bibliography', incorrect and unfortunate as it may be, is here to stay and the situation must be accepted.

There is, however, still current a frequent wish to try to reserve the term bibliography for what may increasingly be regarded the scholarly or 'scientific' study of books. Much of the writing about books, quite apart from those who write of the contents of books, is basically emotional rather than scientific. This is not to denigrate such writing, much of which is extremely valuable. It is, however, of a different order from what is now regarded as bibliography and is, by analogy, best called 'book-lore', but nowadays, more commonly called bibliophily. Be-fore the days of the new bibliography few writers felt the need to distinguish in this manner. Thus Emerson was thinking essentially of the bibliophilic approach to books when writing of of the Roxburgh sale. 'The annals of bibliography afford many examples of the delirious extent to which book-fancying can go, when the legitimate delight in a book is transferred to a rare edition or to a manuscript. This mania reached its height about the beginning of the present century.' Isaac Disraeli, on the other hand, had felt the need to coin the word 'bibliognost' to indicate a somewhat similar enthusiasm.

The difficulty which is experienced in tracing the history of the group of words which have been used for these related activities is some indication of the change in bibliographical studies. The present position is, in fact, almost precisely the opposite of the situation as it appeared up to the end of the nineteenth century. Before that time a group of loosely related studies were known by a number of ill-defined and changing terms. Now one term, or at the most two if 'bibliophily' is also accepted as current, is an general use. Although the word itself has now passed out of the area of controversy the same is not true of its meaning. Over the century and a half which separates us from the time of Dibdin, definition has followed definition and gradually something of a pattern has emerged. The special emphasis within bibliographical studies at a particular period has, of necessity, been reflected in the definitions of the time. Whatever have been the varying interpretations of the past, the starting point now must be the most satisfying of the modern definitions.

In 1945 the Bibliographical Society published its commemorative volume *The Bibliographical Society, 1892–1942. Studies in Retrospect.*[1] The key to the subject was contributed by Sir Walter Greg in his chapter entitled 'Bibliography – a retrospect'.[2] In this, Sir Walter wrote, 'to avoid ambiguity I would define "bibliography" to mean the study of books as material objects. The qualification is important. It is a sort of filioque clause directed against a particular heresy; one which is or has been widespread, is still popular, but is in my opinion none the less damnable. It seems obvious that I may study the Book of Genesis, or the *Odyssey*, or *The Laws of Ecclesiastical Polity*, or *The Origin of Species*, or *The Bad Child's Book of Beasts*, and never come within a hundred miles of bibliography, because bibliography has nothing whatever to do with the subject or literary content of the book.'[3] There is no better starting point for a

[1] *The Bibliographical Society. The Bibliographical Society, 1892–1942. Studies in Retrospect.* London. 1945.

(hereafter referred to as: *Studies in Retrospect*)

[2] *GREG*, W. W. 'Bibliography – a retrospect'. *Studies in Retrospect*. pp. 23–31.

[3] *Studies in Retrospect*. p. 24.

discussion of the function of bibliography than Greg's emphasis on the study of the book as a physical object and there is no more important qualification to be borne in mind than the final phrase of the extract quoted which disallowed the connection between bibliography and the literary or subject content of the book.

This statement has the seeds of possible disagreement. The aspect of literary content with which bibliography has no connection is that of critical evaluation. According to A. S. F. Gow, A. E. Housman in the course of his unpublished Inaugural Lecture at Cambridge in 1911, said that 'a scholar. . . had no more concern with the merits of the literature with which he deals than Linnaeus or Newton with the beauties of the countryside or of the starry heavens'.[1] It is in this respect that bibliography is divorced from the book's content, but a thread of connections exist which Greg had stressed in an earlier article.

Greg's 1945 definition was destined to be the last of the several statements on the subject which he had made throughout his life. Even though his ideas changed, and sometimes radically, there are basic and obvious connections between all the variations. No one could doubt but that it was the same mind at work evolving his theories with that exactness which was typical of all Greg's work. All Greg's definitions will be referred to later, but, at the moment, it is the qualification in his 1932 Presidential Address which is important. He then wrote, 'At the root of all literary criticism lies the question of transmission, and it is bibliography that enables us to deal with the problem'[2] and later on in the same paper, 'Books are the material means by which literature is transmitted; therefore bibliography, the study of books, is essentially the science of the transmission of literary documents.'[3] Greg also gave renewed life to an older saying of Copinger,

[1] *GOW*, A. S. F. *A. E. Housman.* Cambridge University Press. 1936. p. 34.

[2] *The Library*: Fourth Series. Vol. XIII (1932–33). p. 113.

[3] *ibid.* p. 115.

that 'bibliography is the grammar of literary investigation.'[1]

Literature and literary documents are, obviously, far from forgotten or disregarded as part of the function of bibliography. Whereas literary history and criticism are concerned with the history and evaluation of the text itself, bibliography transfers its interests to the study of the material means of the transmission of the texts.

In essence the problem resolves itself into something which is quite simple. Books, in the sense in which Greg applied the term, must be interpreted as inclusive of all those material objects on which ideas were communicated by means of a record which was designed to be, if not permanent, at least lasting. He was even prepared, in 1945, to leave the question open for future discussion as to 'whether a phonographic record is a book'.[2]

There have been times when men had to be content that the expression of their ideas should be entirely transitory and vanish with their voices. On other occasions, through the media of increasingly sophisticated inventions, they have been able to make speech itself achieve a measure of permanence. On still other occasions, and these provide the bulk of the material with which bibliography has had to concern itself up to the present, they have utilized whatever physical means were appropriate to their time and the standard of the civilization in which they lived. Cave paintings; baked clay tablets; papyrus rolls; vellum, parchment and paper manuscripts; movable type printing; all these have in the past, for varying periods, provided the material objects by means of which men have communicated with their fellows from whom they have been separated by space or time or both. As time goes by, the modern inventive mind multiplies these media and the bibliographical picture becomes increasingly complicated.

---

[1] *ibid.* p. 114.

Copinger's original text appeared in his Presidential Address of 1892 (*Transactions of the Bibliographical Society*. Vol. 1. p. 34).

[2] *Studies in Retrospect.* p. 25n.

Although bibliography is concerned with the physical problems and aspects of such material, there is little to be gained, apart from purely antiquarian pleasure, in unravelling such problems for their own sake. The major interest will always lie in some relationship to the text which is being transmitted. The bibliographer's interest in manuscripts lies fundamentally in the text which the manuscripts contain; his concern with printed books as physical objects is in order that he may the better understand the text contained within them. The function of bibliography resolves itself into the consideration of the relationship of all these forms of related material to each other.

Every book, whatever its text may contain, begins as an idea in an author's mind. Up to that moment bibliography is not involved. The moment comes when the author sets down these ideas on paper, his manuscript is created, and it is the first item to have any bibliographical significance. Probably from that manuscript the first printed text will be made. Bibliography will then become concerned with the physical problems of those copies individually, with the relationship of all the copies of that first printing to each other and their relationship to the manuscript from which they all sprang. As months and years and generations go by later printings will be based sometimes upon earlier printings, sometimes upon the original manuscripts and sometimes based very largely upon the editorial interpretation of what the author might conceivably have written. The province of bibliography is to attempt to understand and explain the complex relationship which now exists between perhaps dozens of printings, thousands of copies and the probably small number of extant manuscripts and, above everything else, to relate this all to the text which it was the author's original intention to have written.

The field of bibliography is so wide and, at first glance, so ill-defined that it has to be regarded in its constituent parts if it is to have any significance as a whole. Since these parts are so closely inter-related, it is difficult to think of them in evolutionary terms with the neat structure of a family tree. Rather do they appear as points around a circle in which each aspect is supported by all its neighbours, but in varying degrees according to the emphasis of a particular piece of work. The nomenclature of the divisions or areas of bibliography has varied over the years in a manner not dissimilar from those which were concerned with the general name itself. It differs, however, in that there is now less agreement over the naming of the parts than of the whole. Fredson Bowers is scarcely a sufficiently conformist figure in the world of bibliography for his definition of the parts to secure wide and general agreement. On the other hand no one else has provided such a useful starting point for the trail which, as Lawrence Wroth wrote, 'leads far'.

In the current printings of the *Encyclopaedia Britannica*, Bowers has written, '. . . in modern times the word bibliography is ordinarily associated with two sets of activities: (1) enumerative (or systematic) bibliography, the listing according to some system or reference scheme of books that have a formal relationship; and (2) analytical (or critical) bibliography, the examination of books as tangible objects with a view to the recovery of the details of the physical process of their manufacture, and the analysis of the effect of this production process on the physical characteristics of any specific copy of a book.

'Analytical bibliography can be pursued independently of any limited objective; that is, it may be studied as a pure discipline concerned with recovering and interpreting evidence about production processes as preserved in the physical features of books of various periods. The application of such information, however, usually takes the form of (a) descriptive bibliography; or (b) textual bibliography.'[1] In Bowers' many writings since the first appearance of this text his viewpoint has not changed radically so far as this small part of the article was concerned. Any dispute which has ranged around Bowers' writings has been much less because of his division of the subject field than because of the weight which he has given to some of the parts.

---

[1] Article under 'Bibliography' in printings from 1959 onwards.

The strictly enumerative aspect of bibliography has never seriously been called in doubt so far as its general function is concerned. The scope and methodology of enumeration is, however, in the throes of revolution. For so long the desirable ends of enumerative bibliography have seemed to be an impossible pipe-dream. Now the impossible may, truly, only be that which takes a little longer. At least, it is sufficiently feasible to make it worth while thinking out afresh what the role of enumeration really is in bibliography. On the other hand, analytical bibliography is still in process of being thought out for the first time and has no public image to change. Here, Greg's study of the physical nature of the book becomes the most detailed. It is a study which is still within its first century of life and has gained in complexity throughout each decade. The bounds of analytical bibliography are impossible to define because the potential of new weapons in the armoury is unknown. In the broadest and most general terms it consists in discovering and explaining every fact about the 'means of transmission' from the manuscripts to the finished product. It covers what Ferguson termed the 'biography of the book'.

In bibliography, as in many subjects, the great foundation study is historical. It is impossible to assess how a text has developed in relation to the materials of transmission unless the sequence of operations which produced that material object are well known. This entails a study of manuscript transmission, the methods of printing, of house practice at various periods, the background of publishing, of printing, of authorship, of bookselling. All of these are facets of which the bibliographer must be aware if he is to have any success in solving the problems of transmission. The background of historical bibliography is the one against which all other matters must be viewed. The historical sense serves to remind that manuscript studies are a part of bibliography even though they have tended to create a separate area of study. Historical bibliographical studies are particularly subject to bifurcation. Palaeography is increasingly becoming distinct from bibliography, papyrology is a study almost completely on its own and others are likely to grow so. This is not to be impulsively regretted since specialized studies can advance in no other way, but synthesis becomes increasingly important and dishearteningly more difficult.

Bowers has always placed great stress on his opinion that analytical bibliography is a subject which can be pursued as an entirely independent area of study for its own sake alone. It is, he has averred, a discipline of its own and can be treated as such. On the other hand, he has given equal stress to the two chief uses which have normally been made of such analytical work. Descriptive bibliography has long been acknowledged as one primary field of bibliographical activity and greeted especially warmly by those who wish to see a strictly utilitarian end for these studies. Once the idea of enumerative bibliography has been accepted, it is no great step to descriptive work which places increasing stress on the bibliographical problems of the items described. What is not always so readily grasped is that, as analytical studies have been more refined, so descriptive bibliographical work has developed to the stage at which it bears little relationship at all to enumerative work. In its early days the connection was not difficult to establish; now increasingly, it is. The other end product which Bowers has stressed is the one with which he has been most closely identified personally and which is more controversial and less liable to general acceptance. For the past fifty or so years increasing stress has been laid on the relationship between the bibliographical aspects of a work and the understanding of the text. Some critics regard it as unfortunate that the term textual bibliography has come to be applied to this branch of the study but, nevertheless, this is the term by which it is most generally known. Since, in Greg's phrase, books are the 'material means by which literature is transmitted', then it seems not illogical to suggest that a close study of the materials may throw some light on the history of the text. Rather than textual bibliography it may perhaps be better to regard it as bibliography applied to the problems of textual studies, but, however it is regarded and however it is labelled, it is an area of bibliographical study which is currently extremely lively and on behalf of which many important claims are being made.

Useful as Bowers' analysis of the field of bibliography is it would be wrong to suggest that other patterns do not exist. Many writers have been concerned to make a clear distinction between those areas of bibliography which concern themselves more or less directly with the subject matter of books and those which do not. The chief point of issue is usually the bibliographical analysis of the subject contents rather than any textual problems, and, therefore, such work is usually associated with enumerative problems. The first edition of the *Encyclopedia Americana*, for example, in 1830, began its definition of bibliography, 'but in its modern and more extended sense, it signifies the knowledge of books, in reference to the subjects discussed in them. . . . It is, therefore, divided into two branches, the first of which has reference to the contents of books, and may be called for want of a better phrase, *intellectual bibliography*; the second treats of their external character, the history of particular copies, etc., and may be termed *material bibliography*.' A division of this kind has been a basic requirement for many decades, especially by librarians and by scholars in many subjects. Here the comprehensive and exhaustive treatment of books by 'pure' bibliographers has not produced the kind of tool which they most regularly require. What these groups want is something which it is not easy to describe; it is something more tutelary than the majority of subject bibliographies and something more comprehensive than most literature guides.

The most recent plea for a classification of bibliography along these lines has been by Lloyd Hibberd.[1] His suggestion was for the term 'reference bibliography' to cover the old conception of intellectual bibliography and what is now more generally known as enumerative or systematic bibliography. In Hibberd's words, 'it begins with simple systematic compilation but

[1] *HIBBERD*, Lloyd. 'Physical and reference bibliography'. *The Library*: Fifth Series. Vol. XX (1965). pp. 124–134.

proceeds by searching for new sources and by producing various classified lists (pilot works). It is aimed at the librarian, the general scholar, and the layman requiring data on a subject.' The emphasis is entirely on the book or the materials as a means of conveying ideas and information; the problems of the physical nature of the book itself do not loom very large. When the physical nature of the book itself is the aspect on which the major amount of study is likely to be lavished, then Hibberd suggested 'physical bibliography'. Within this heading would be included all that Bowers described as analytical, descriptive and textual.

The attraction in thinking in terms such as intellectual and material or reference and physical is that they so closely relate to the use being made of the studies. The disadvantage, but one which applies equally to any other division, is in the tendency to separate the parts of an area of study in which all the specializations rely so heavily upon each other. Whatever the final results of nomenclature may be, however, the general tendency of an investigation into the functioning of a subject area is to increase the awareness of the interdependence of each of the parts upon the whole.

If Greg's basic definition of bibliography is allied to any attempt to distinguish the parts of the whole, it provides a perfect framework for the more detailed study of the role of bibliography. Books can be studied as physical, or as Bowers wrote, tangible objects and from this study, important relationships can be shown to exist between books and also between copies of the same book. Bowers' definition, above all else, stresses the variety of purposes served by this study and the range of its general functions.

This variety has not been an entirely mixed blessing over the years. As specialization within the various fields of bibliography has grown more acute, so has a tendency grown up to work in that particular field in ignorance – and occasionally disdain – of the related studies. Bibliography will only be in a really healthy condition so long as the 'study of the material book' continues to have some unifying principle and practice. We have been told once, in clear and forthright terms, what it is which we need.

In his Presidential Address to the Bibliographical Society in 1932, Greg wrote, '. . . let it be understood that it (bibliography) is in no way particularly or primarily concerned with the enumeration or description of books – a belief which has done much in the past to reduce it to futility and retard the recognition of its real nature and importance.'[1] Later in the same year, Sir Stephen Gaselee registered his complete disagreement with this viewpoint and devoted the whole of his Presidential Address to an analysis of the role of systematic bibliography in the development of scholarship.

When Gaselee's address was printed, A. W. Pollard added an important note.[2] He made no attempt to adjudicate between these rival points of view but, standing by his new position, said, 'I was far from forging chains for bibliography, but demanding for it the cat's freedom to walk by itself. . . Dr Greg, in what seems to me excessive concern to prove that the study for which he has done so much is worthy of the name of a science, has given, I think, rather undue pre-eminence to an aspect of it which until lately was regarded as a department of 'criticism', 'textual' or 'higher'. I have done something myself to claim 'criticism' of this kind as a province of bibliography. But, as Mr Gaselee has kindly noted, the historical import of bibliography in which enumeration plays a special part attracts me and I should regret the acceptance of any new definition of our study which may tend to ignore, or depreciate it. Fortunately, the question appears to be almost entirely one of definition, and there seems to be no dispute as to what should or should not be done. Dr Greg during his Presidentship did his utmost to procure help for making a start with a special catalogue of English books from 1641 to 1700, and Mr Gaselee is far too good a classic to be indifferent to the study of the transmission of texts.

[1] *The Library*: Fourth Series. Vol. XIII (1932–33). p. 114.
[2] *ibid.* pp. 225–58.

We all want the same things: the question at issue is as to whether we want them *as bibliographers,* or in some other capacity. My own preference is for "a big umbrella".'

This was not the only occasion on which Pollard's cool, clear voice was heard calling for reason in these matters. All bibliographical work, if well done, is of value and has a profound, if not always direct, result on other areas of the same study. There is no need to wander from Greg's basic definition; but Pollard's injunction to remember the importance of the whole, even for those who are working in one highly specialized area, is particularly relevant today. All studies in bibliography are studies under the big umbrella. What we need to be able to do is to understand as exactly as possible what each area of study keeps before it as its objective and how each of the parts are related to the whole.

2

Enumerative bibliography

Ever since the time when books began to be produced in quantity and the book trade and librarianship began to emerge with clear-cut functions, there has been some kind of need for a purely enumerative listing of the items concerned. The nature of librarianship dictated the particular needs of that profession, which were experienced more critically at an earlier stage than in other areas of the book world. A library alone had the problem of dealing with a collection of books, which was not only frequently a large one at the outset, but also one which was constantly increasing. The earliest library catalogues were essentially examples of enumerative work since this provided all the detail which was necessary.

The Alexandrian library provides one of the outstanding examples of this type of work and recognition of the importance was undoubtedly the factor which led, as Sir Stephen Gaselee pointed out, to the emergence as bibliographers of the Alexandrian's earliest librarians. It was at that time the prime function of a librarian and the full catalogue of the Alexandrian library, if extant, would have provided a bibliographical tool of incalculable historical importance. The holocaust of the library destroyed so much material that it has served to increase our sense of loss at not having even a record of the titles. At all periods from the Greek world to the modern world the contribution of libraries to the business of enumerative bibliography has been considerable and it is now one of the factors which must be considered.

Enumerative bibliography is the easiest of all the particular areas of the study to understand. This is largely because it meets most accurately all that is generally required by the lay public, a straightforward listing of books and without the burdening of over-much detail. Having collected the material the importance of its systematizing becomes obvious and this area of bibliography is just as happily called 'systematic' as 'enumerative'. There are, however, certain particular problems in the organization of this bibliographical record and these will be dealt with separately in Chapter Five on the arrangement of bibliographies.

The basic idea of enumerative bibliography, therefore, raises no problems since its overall function is clear, the listing of the salient details about a particular group of books which have some kind of co-ordinating factor. A number of other issues, however, which are equally as pertinent to a full understanding of the whole subject, are more controversial.

In the 'Bibliography – a retrospect' chapter already referred to, Greg placed particular stress on the fact that a bibliography, of any kind, was an uncritical listing of items without reference to the subject matter or quality of the book. 'There are still some who cling to the belief that a bibliographer is somehow concerned with the literary content of the books he examines, that it is within his province to determine and analyse, even to appraise and criticize, that content. It is a curious heresy, for one would have thought it obvious that the criticism of works on any particular subject was the business of an expert in that subject, and however able bibliographers may be they would hardly claim to be universal experts. The error has of course arisen through the use of the expression "a bibliography" to mean a list of books on some particular subject and the assumption that "a bibliographer" is primarily a compiler of "bibliographies". It is natural enough that the misapprehension should be a popular one, since it is convenient to the students of any

subject to regard bibliographers as a race of useful drudges –
servi a bibliotheca – who are there to do for them some of the
spade work that they are too lazy or too incompetent to do for
themselves. It is less easy to understand why bibliographers
should have been so ready to accept this ancillary position. I
suppose the answer is that it has often happened that they themselves began by being interested in the literature of some particular subject, and became bibliographers in their endeavour
to collect and describe the books belonging to that particular
field of study. Such was certainly my own experience. Most of
what I know of bibliography I have learned through the study
of books to which I was led by an interest in Elizabethan drama.
Of course if a "bibliography" is to include any detailed description of the books themselves (apart from their literary content)
the compiler will need to possess some bibliographical knowledge or else obtain the assistance of a bibliographical expert.
But that does not alter the fact that the compilation of the
"bibliography" itself – the selection of the works and their
arrangement in the most illuminating order, as well as any
comment or criticism it may be proposed to include – must be
the work of the expert in the subject with which it deals and not
of the bibliographer. For my own part I very early recognized
that, however much I might need the results of bibliographical
research in compiling a list of English plays, bibliography itself
was something very different from the literary compilation on
which I was engaged.'[1]

Greg insisted upon this important distinction between bibliographical and non-bibliographical work throughout his long
career and was joined by others who fought, what still seems to
be, a losing battle. If bibliography is concerned with the
material or physical nature of the books and not with the literary
or subject content, then it follows that no question of exclusion
of items from the listing can be entertained on grounds
of quality or importance. A bibliography, if it is to be

[1] *Studies in Retrospect.* pp. 24–25.

properly so-called, must be comprehensive and not selective.

Conflicting interests, together with the realization of the difficulties of comprehensive coverage, however right and desirable, have kept this as a live issue throughout the whole development of the studies in the subject.

Conrad Gesner, the so-called 'father of bibliography' was imbued by this instinct when he published his *Bibliotheca Universalis* in 1545, but, in accord with the general spirit of his age, he could not have thought that he was abandoning the principle when he ignored the vernacular and listed only those books written in Latin, Greek and Hebrew. Each generation has chosen, through ignorance or a desire for simplicity, to ignore those items which seem to be outside the range of the list. Manuscript material is frequently excluded, foreign language material disappears from popular listings, recordings are often not regarded as 'book' material and, consequently, left out of a 'bibliography'. It is hardly surprising, therefore, that Gesner, when producing a comprehensive list, should have ignored works which, because of their vernacular text, could be considered as 'writ in water'. The desire to be able to produce a complete listing of the world's literature has been a day dream of bibliographers ever since and the modern bibliographer's insistence on the uncritical nature of the listing has strengthened this feeling very considerably.

Irrespective of the desirability or practicability of such a scheme, there have been those who felt that concentration upon bibliographical minutiae had led bibliographers astray from what they should have regarded as their main duty; namely, the preparation of bibliographical guides and surveys. The demand for this kind of enumerative bibliography has been particularly strong from librarians, the nature of whose work requires such tools. Early in this present century, in 1903, James Duff Brown voiced the concern of some librarians at the activities of bibliographers and their apparently all-consuming concern with bibliographical pedantry.

This attack of Brown's, together with the reply which it

invoked deserves careful attention because it brought the conflicting attitudes into proper focus. Brown's paper appeared in
The Library without any apparently immediate cause.[1] Although this was a time at which many of Greg's and McKerrow's
highly critical reviews of badly edited texts were appearing and
causing considerable comment, it seemed not to be these
activities of which Brown disapproved. His target was much
more the incunabulists upon whose efforts the whole of modern
bibliographical work had been founded. His displeasure was
because they were not providing the kind of tools for which
Brown personally, and many of his colleagues, felt a need. 'So
much has been written on the subject of Bibliography in all its
aspects that it may seem a little presumptuous on the part of one
who has no claim to be considered a "learned bibliographer",
to intrude on the sacred preserve so long monopolized by a
special class of students and librarians. It is, however, the
privilege of the outsider, not only to see most of the game, but,
being a non-combatant, also to have breath and self-possession
enough to give calm utterance to his opinions on the show. As
a librarian of many years' standing, I have watched the progress of bibliographical work with a great deal of interest, and
I have been especially impressed by the attempts of our English
workers in the field. As the result of this close watching, I feel
in a position to air my views on the whole subject of English
bibliographical work, and I shall do so quite frankly, even at
the risk of repeating statements which have already been better
put by more qualified writers.

'Without further preface, then, I may mention as a first point,
that I believe English bibliographical work to be little better
than a hollow sham, carried out on the narrowest possible lines,
by men who are more anxious for personal glory or profit than
the accomplishment of any work of public utility. Indeed, it
may be safely said that modern bibliography is exactly the
same old egotistical hobby which it was a hundred years ago,

[1] *The Library*: N. S. Vol. IV (1903). pp. 144–162.

when it became a fad for rich collectors, and the dry-as-dust devotees of fifteenth-century Latinity. Everyone who has any-thing to do with books, is interested in the incunabula and old literature generally, and so far as the accurate recording of rare and valuable books is concerned, anyone can sympathize with what may be termed the bibliographical side of literary history. But it is when this kind of research, confined to one narrow period, and on one particular system, is pursued simply as a dilettante fad, without any object of utility, that the prac-tical mind revolts, and demands a change, or rest. For years past the world has been waiting for some practical outcome of all this wonderful bibliographical study, of which so much has been heard, but nothing has appeared save more studies of the incunabula rearranged to give an appearance of novelty. It is a remarkable thing that bibliographers are unable to tear themselves away from the typographical mysteries of the fif-teenth century, and that they should spend all their time squabbling about type-founts and the merely material side of books, when so much remains to be done to elucidate the history of the book during periods even more interesting, and certainly more influential from the literary point of view. We have elaborate lists of the incunabula arranged in order of the author's names; then someone comes along and rearranges these lists under the names of towns, and the names of the printers. Not satisfied with this, another group of workers devote themselves to the incunabula contained in particular libraries, and then comes the chronological order crank. One man confines himself to the presses of particular printers or towns; and another exploits the type. Again, we have the patriotic biographer who makes the nationality of printing in the fifteenth century his mark, and so the farce goes on, till the incunabula have been exploited off the face of the earth.

'Meanwhile, amidst this laborious industry, the world is waiting to know what the fifteenth-century books were all *about*. Can any of the learned bibliographers who have wasted years collecting title-pages and colophons and collations, and even specimens, just give us a glimmer of light on the contents of the books which interested the people of the fifteenth century? What were their popular poetry, fiction, philosophy, art, and other studies? What are these books *about*, with the queer Latin, German, French, Italian, Dutch, and English titles? Literary historians do not enlighten us much about individual books, and it seems to be reserved for the bibliographer to supply the missing descriptions, only he is so busy quarrelling over *blank leaves* and questions of dimensions, that he has no time to ascertain the contents of the books which pass through his hands. Thus arises the popular belief that bibliographers are generally ignorant of the contents of books, and thus, also, we get at the kernel of the saying: "The librarian who reads is lost." This latter is but a bibliographer's way of stating that the book-collator's attention must be strictly confined to the *blank leaves* and the signatures. He must not glance at the literary contents – that is reserved for some other department of human activity, which, strangely enough, does not seem to exist; as both bibliographers and literary historians repudiate the idea of book annotation.

'It is a great point in modern bibliographical science, to make a careful note of the *blank leaves*. Many a book is imperfect which lacks them, and its market value may be seriously impaired if a blank leaf, completing a section, is absent. Heavens! what a depth of scientific accuracy and observation is implied in the careful description of a blank leaf, and how the integrity of the literary contents of a book must suffer if its waste papers are missing! It is the same with margins, and other points connected with material condition. In short, the modern scientific bibliographer is a kind of hack for the secondhand bookseller and book-collector. Years of devotion expended on the study of book values, rarity, odd physical characteristics, antiquity, and uniqueness, have made the bibliographer a mere hanger-on at the heels of the curiosity hunter and book dealer. His knowledge is expended chiefly on that side of the history and contents of the printed book, which is valueless to all save a few interested collectors, and he has neglected to leave any complete or general information concerning the subject-matter of books. But it is not only the individual bibliographer who has neglected the vital part of bibliography. Nearly the whole of the bibliographical societies are working on the same narrow lines. Instead of useful subject bibliographies, we are fobbed off with monographs in illustration of the special hobbies of individual members. One crank compiles a monograph on the quads and quoins used by Aldus, and the society forthwith prints it in a strictly limited edition with the ulterior view of creating a famine, and so in time causing the publications of the society to rank among the world's book rarities. This ambition would be legitimate enough if these societies were private book-publishing clubs like the Bannatyne, Roxburghe, or Spalding: but they are nothing of the sort. They profess to deal with bibliographical science on the broadest possible lines; they invite public libraries and the general public to become members; and they do not undertake to confine themselves to obscure little points in historical typography which may chance to interest one or two of the purely antiquarian members. Their appeal is, on the contrary, very much wider, but they do not stand by their principles and compile and issue works which would be of use to the public at large. There is not a single bibliographical society in existence which makes the slightest attempt to justify its existence as a useful institution, by publishing acceptable work of general interest, and it has been left for an American library association to point the way. On the one hand we have professing *Bibliographical* societies printing a number of expensive, and comparatively useless monographs on petty aspects of historical typography; while, on the other hand, we have a society which only professes to be a *Library* association, issuing valuable *bibliographical* indexes to history, fine arts, periodicals, and other departments of knowledge. The contrast is very marked, and it proves that we must not look to professional bibliographers for any assistance in the work of recording, indexing, and annotating the literature of all times.

'Without necessarily adopting the extravagantly wide definitions of Bibliography adopted by Peignot and other authors,
whose industry was scarcely equal to their ambition, it has
always seemed to me that Bibliography meant more than the
mere physical description of books and the record of their
monetary values. The value of detailed registration of pages,
signatures, watermarks, sizes by paper-folds or centimetres,
blank leaves, and all the other etceteras of exact collation, never
struck me as being more than a dreadful waste of time, save as
regards very old books, which cannot be described satisfactorily
without the use of such a system. It may also serve as a kind of
testimonial to the honesty of a bookseller, and a guarantee to
the purchaser that he is getting all he finds described; but to
see bibliographers seriously quoting such scraps of the obvious,
in the case of comparatively modern books, regularly paged
and easily identified, is really a solemn sham. It is an endeavour
to provide with a series of formidable looking symbols a simple
art which would be ever so much more rational if stripped of
all this pseudo-scientific garnishing.

'Instead of wasting more time wandering about the by-ways
of mediaeval literature and typography, our living "learned
bibliographers" and bibliographical societies should devote
some of their surplus energy to the advancement of real learning
in its widest sense, by providing students of all kinds with complete or selective bibliographies of every useful subject, properly
annotated and indexed. The day has gone past for all the
bibliographical work to be undertaken in the interests of the
Dominie Sampsons and Snuffy Davies of the private library
and the public book-barrow, and it is time a little more attention was bestowed on the actual needs of living people. In
particular the incunabula require a long rest, unless some bibliographer will now set to work and provide us with a complete
subject-index to the literature of the fifteenth century? There
are hundreds of subjects requiring treatment, and if, instead of
publishing monographs on printing presses, whose productions
are so rare as to be seldom seen by bibliographers and never by

the general public, our bibliographers would quit the path of dilettantism for that of practical work, they would not only enhance the value of their own work, but would be of enormous assistance to students the world over, and even to ordinary seekers of everyday information. Bibliography should be understood properly to include the books of all times and on all topics, and the present narrow view taken by so many, that it is the science relating to old and rare books, should be abandoned. To such a pass has this cult of the mediaeval book come, that it is actually more difficult to trace the works of a living author, than it is to secure a true, full and particular account of the titles of all the books written by some old Latinist. There are great tracts in the long history of English bibliography remaining to be studied and recorded, and this is another direction in which our bibliographers could pursue good and useful work. But it is always the remote and far away subject which attracts English students. They neglect the work lying at home demanding attention, in order to exploit seeming mysteries at a distance which are really as commonplace and unattractive as the home product appears to be by its very familiarity.'

Although this opinion was expressed over sixty years ago, it is by no means outmoded now and it will be assured of a measure of agreement in many quarters. Equally forceful was the reply, in the same issue of the journal from A. W. Pollard.[1] The lapse of time has done nothing here to mitigate the force of his argument which stressed, with all Pollard's cold clarity, the standpoint of the bibliographer in the full sense of the word.

'Since the honour of replying to Mr Brown's interesting article has been offered me, it would be pusillanimous to decline it, but I must own to some trepidation in accepting. With all the advantages of an "outsider" and a "non-combatant", Mr Brown's "calm utterance" has taken the form of denouncing the friends with whom I have the honour to work as "hacks" and "cranks", "hangers-on at the heels of the curiosity-hunter

[1] *ibid.*

34

and book-dealer", pursuers of a "hollow sham" or (variantly) of a "solemn" one, riders of an "egotistical hobby", and cultivators of a "dilettante fad". He has penetrated into the recesses of our minds and has discovered that we are "more anxious for personal glory or profit", than to be of any use, and that collectively in our little societies we entertain "ulterior views" of creating a "book famine", while we are not above using false pretences to lure the innocent librarian and general public into paying us their guineas. If Mr Brown as a calm outsider can be betrayed into these violent expressions, an opponent who does not even pretend to be disinterested must surely pray that no action for libel may follow his attempt to reply.

'Mr Brown's remarks about the bibliographical societies offer, perhaps, as convenient a starting point as can be found. He appears to be under the belief, which is not wholly peculiar to him, that when a society is formed an entirely new motive power is called into existence. Unfortunately this is not the case. If one hundred people form themselves into a society and not one of them is prepared to do any work, the work of that society will be nil. If ninety-five members of the society adopt a purely receptive attitude, and five are ready to work, the work of the society will be the work of those five members. If they all happen to be interested in the same section of their subject, the work of the society will be one-sided. But the fault will not rest with the five members, nor with the governing body of the society for accepting their help. The fault will rest with the other members of the society who do nothing, or with the outsiders who might join the society and work for it, but who prefer to criticize. Only in one case could the blame fairly be shifted to other shoulders. It might conceivably happen that, by ingenious gerrymandering or lawless defiance of the rules, a small clique controlled the work of a society, and refused to print the books of any but its own partisans. Mr Brown appears to know of such a society. It is one managed by so skilful a caucus that it can confine itself to "obscure little points of historical typography which may chance to interest one or two of the purely antiquarian members". The passivity of a society which accepted a succession of books in which only one or two of its members were interested would indeed be wonderful, and it would be more wonderful still if its members steadily increased, and its uninteresting books sold in the outside market at a price considerably higher than that at which members purchased them. This last detail, however, according to Mr Brown, is only the effect of further manipulations. To him it is an offence to regulate the number of copies printed in accordance with the demand. Sweeter, it may be presumed, are the ways of the publisher, who sells the first half of an edition at a very high price, and the second half at a very low one; thus offering to book buyers an instance of how disadvantageous it is for such worms as they to rise early.

'If the view suggested in the foregoing paragraph be correct, Mr Brown's duty is clear, Instead of remaining a philosophic outsider, indulging in language, esoterically, no doubt, calm, but phenomenally, and to mere outward seeming, a little offensive, he should bear his share of the burden of production, for zero, even when multiplied a hundred, or it may be three hundred times, remains zero still, and until men are found to work along new lines of bibliographical research, the present little band of cranks, hacks, hangers-on and faddists have no competitors.

'Here it becomes reasonable to ask if the aforesaid handful of workers are really deserving of the hard names Mr Brown showers on them from the severely practical and utilitarian standpoint which he effects. If the work which any body of men are doing for a society is bad in itself, then it would be well that the society should dissolve rather than continue to print it. If, however, the work is good in itself, it does not become bad because other people who might be doing other work prefer to be idle. Now to the goodness of the work of my antiquarian friends Mr Brown himself bears eloquent, though seemingly unconscious witness. Thanks to their labours, he tells us, it is actually easier "to secure a true, full and particular account of the titles of all the books written by some old latinist" than to trace the works of a living author. Could any testimonial be more emphatic? Only let the other men imitate this zeal and the whole burden will be lifted! Not so, says Mr Brown, these men are the only workers in the field, therefore they must clear the corner of it in which I am interested and leave their own. Mr Brown seems a little peremptory.

'If we pass from the general effect of our antiquaries' toils to some of the details on which Mr Brown fastens, here again he provides his own answer. He is particularly severe on any allusion to blank leaves, even to the point of refusing to mention them, save with the added scorn that appears to be lent by italics. And yet, bye-and-bye, when he is more anxious to use his stick to beat another poor dog, he makes the antiquaries a present of their whole case, owning that "very old books" "cannot be described satisfactorily without the use of such a system" as that which includes "detailed registration of pages, signatures, watermarks, sizes by paper-folds, or centimetres, blank leaves [*sic*], and all the other etceteras of exact collation". I must confess myself to a preference for being told whether even a modern book which begins on the third leaf of a sheet has lost a half-title and a portrait, or only two pieces of white paper; but my brief at present is for the antiquaries, and since Mr Brown himself owns that the books with which they deal cannot be satisfactorily described save on their system, I must conclude that his earlier gibes were only intended to please the "gallery".

'I am reminded by another glance at Mr Brown's paper that "the world" is still "waiting". It is waiting, so Mr Brown assures us, for "some practical outcome" from all this bibliographical work, and more particularly to know what those fifteenth-century books "with queer titles", were all about. I am afraid that Mr Brown has made the mistake of regarding himself and the world as too nearly synonymous. His own generous anxiety to know more about fifteenth-century literature I fully believe in and sympathize with. I may even venture

37

to advertise the new edition of Mr Arber's "English Garner", by mentioning that I have written a preface to one of the volumes, to try to prove that this fifteenth-century literature is not quite so dull as it is usually thought to be. But that the world is waiting to be told about fifteenth-century literature with the smallest approach to impatience is too gross and improbable an imagination to deceive a child.

'But if the world were really waiting, have bibliographers, as such, nothing to tell it? I say, as such, for the true bibliographer, like the cat in Mr Kipling's "Just so" story, ever bargains to walk by himself when all sorts of people are trying to tie him down to stay with them for always and always and always, and do their work. The chemist says "These bibliographers are but drones: they have never made me a bibliography of chemistry." But the chemist must make his own bibliography of chemistry, for he and he only possesses the knowledge of the subject which can make such a bibliography intelligent. The bibliographer can give him many hints about forms and typographical arrangement, and the need for uniformity, but he cannot make the bibliography himself unless he knows chemistry, and if he tries to get up chemistry for the purpose of making the bibliography he courts disaster. Of course one and the same person may be bibliographer and also a chemist, or a chemist and also a bibliographer, and then his bibliography of chemistry ought, alike formally and materially, to be very good indeed. But its material goodness will not proceed from his qualifications as a bibliographer.

'Now apply this doctrine, which is surely sound, to Mr Brown's (or the world's!) desire to know what fifteenth-century books "with their queer titles" are about. Is a mere bibliographer to summarize a whole European literature – theology, law, medicine, philosophy, the attempts at science, as well as all those subjects, such as history, which seem easier to handle than they are, because they have a less special terminology? If Mr Brown's lectures on Bibliography at the School of Economics taught his hearers how to describe books on subjects of which they are ignorant, my regret that I could not manage to go to any of them is immeasurably increased. But I am afraid that not even he could accomplish such a feat.

'Yet it would appear from Mr Brown's article that our American friends have already shown us how these things may be done. With a suppression of an essential fact which I cannot admire, he holds up the American Library Association as having done the work which bibliographers have left undone – the suppressed fact being, that as regards the descriptive catalogue of American history and other already published books, the generosity of Mr George Iles made it possible to carry the work through, with the help of many experts, and that as regards any schemes which the Association may now have in hand, it has them in hand because Mr Carnegie has placed £20,000 at its disposal for the purpose. In so far as these schemes bear good fruit they will do so by securing the help of experts in different subjects to make bibliographies, not by turning bibliographers on to subjects of which they have no competent knowledge, and which they can only illustrate by cutting out snippets from reviews.

'What then is the business of the bibliographer? Primarily and essentially, I should say, the enumeration of books. His is the lowly task of finding out what books exist, and thereby helping to secure their preservation, and furnishing the specialist with information as to the extent of the subject-matter with which he has to deal. In one of the unlucky phrases into which his love of rhetoric betrays him, Mr Brown speaks of the "farce" of different re-arrangements going on "till the incunabula have been exploited off the face of the earth". The truth is, of course, exactly the opposite, every fresh re-arrangement bringing to light more books, and further elucidating their history. "It is a good thing to read books", wrote Frederick Locker, "and it need not be a bad thing to write them; but it is a pious thing to preserve those that have been some time written: the collecting, and mending, and binding, and cataloguing of books are all means to such an end." The more attention is bestowed on

39

any class of book the more (alas) prices rise, and the more incentive there is to bring new copies to light. When the bibliographer has brought books to light and printed lists of them, whether chronologically, if that be his "crank", or under their authors, I submit that he has done a great part of what can reasonably be expected of him. The further treatment of the books so as to show their importance in their several subjects must necessarily be the work of specialists, and cannot usefully be undertaken by anyone else. That the specialists are deplorably slow is only too true, so slow that bibliographers may easily be forgiven if they make raids into subjects for whose treatment they are only inadequately equipped. But this cannot alter the radical principle on which the work must be divided between the two sets of men.

'I said just now that when a bibliographer has enumerated all the books of any period he has done a great part of what can reasonably be expected of him. With the space which remains at my disposal I cannot develop fully my conception of what remains over when this great part has been accomplished, but it may at least be roughly indicated. Mr Brown, with his rather truculent narrowness, jeers at my friend Mr Proctor as a "crank" who "compiles a monograph on the quads and quoins used by Aldus". Now it is Mr Proctor's honourable distinction that instead of, as most of us are content to do, stating any case he may have to expound according to vague general impressions, he puts his facts definitely and concretely, and thus does his work once and for all. Many people knew vaguely that the earliest Greek founts were very complicated. By the simple statement that one of them (not owned by Aldus) contained some 1,350 different "sorts", Mr Proctor demonstrated how, despite the wrong ideals with which the printers started, and the innate conservatism of scholars, the burden laid upon the compositors was so intolerable that it was bound to work its own remedy. Hence the curious history of Greek type, which starting with an attempt at the slavish imitation of handwriting, continually simplified itself without any reference to good models, until it attained the curiously artificial character with which we are familiar. Mr Proctor's monograph on "The Printing of Greek in the Fifteenth Century" does not tell us what the Greek Psalter or "Batrachomyomachia" or the works of Aristotle are "about", but it does give the clue to the difficulties, essential and accidental, which have beset Greek printing from its infancy, and in doing this takes us an important step on the way to overcoming them. If bibliographers help to improve modern printing, they will prove themselves much more useful persons than Mr Brown would allow, and that their work tends in this direction can hardly be denied.

'In a like manner it would be easy to show, though the argument cannot here be developed fully, that both the historian of literature and the critical editor must rely greatly on the help of bibliographers if they are to do justice to their subjects, and avoid serious errors. Unless the bibliographer gives us some inkling of the number of copies which usually made up an edition in early times, and of the frequency with which one edition was succeeded by another, what guide have we to the literary influence and popularity of any given book? Or again, into what useless disquisitions have not critical editors plunged in order to demonstrate the priority of one Prayer Book, or text of any other popular work over another, regardless of the probablility that, owing to the slowness of pulling impressions at a hand-press, books for which a large sale was expected were set up simultaneously at two or more presses, so that two or more editions may have equal claims to priority! Regardless of the trouble they were creating for these blameless critical editors, the printers, it seems certain, used to mix sheets from two different presses at haphazard, and to the innocent scholar each several combination of these different sheets appears as a separate edition. Once more, the part which the compositor might play in creating different "editions" was hardly even guessed until Mr Wynne Baxter suggested it a few months ago. The wiser sort spoke mysteriously of no two copies of an early book being exactly alike, and of "corrections" introduced while books were passing through the press. We had visions of authors picking up damp sheets in printing offices, and stopping the press to set right an error. Who of us imagined that in two cases out of three the "corrector" was only the pressman, whose inking-balls had caught up a few letters out of the forme, and who put them back, or any others he chanced to find on the floor, in what order seemed good to him, and thus created variants which set all critical ingenuity at defiance?

'I hope some day to develop more fully the suggestions of the last paragraph, and others of a like nature. Here it may suffice to point out that so long as literature in order to be communicated has to take material form, so long will it be to the advantage of the little world which cares for literature that every point which concerns this material form should be carefully and thoroughly investigated. It may even be that an examination of the "quads and quoins of Aldus" may possess as much real literary interest as a new disquisition on the relations of Shelley and Harriet Westbrook, or whether George IV did or did not behave shabbily to Sheridan on his death-bed. All knowledge is good, and though we have a right, and even a duty, to condemn those who set others to tasks of which the possible result seems incommensurate to the certain labour, on the other hand, where the work is voluntarily and joyously undertaken, what wise man will be so overbold as to fetter the worker's liberty? Mr Brown has sinned against one of the soundest of maxims, the maxim that tells never to try to pull another man off his hobby. I have pointed out already that to start on indiscriminate annotation of fifteenth-century books is not without danger, but for annotated catalogues, viewed as Mr Brown's special hobby, I have all possible respect and goodwill. It is only when he tries to pull me off my own mount, and my friends off theirs, in order to make us all ride the beasts he offers us, whither he is pleased to direct, that I join issue. Let him annotate and describe what books he pleases, and I will applaud his zeal. Let him start a Descriptive Cataloguing Society, and if I can rake up a spare guinea he shall have it. But when with a humorous assumption of impartiality he denounces work in which he does not happen to be interested as a "sham" ("hollow" or otherwise) and a "dilettante fad" and those who put their hand to it, without fee or reward, as "hacks" and "cranks", then my sympathy with Mr Brown is inclined to cool.'

The plea which James Duff Brown made for greater emphasis on the subject approach to books is an entirely reasonable one and few people are in a better position to realize this need than librarians. At a Library Association Conference in 1936, almost exactly half-way between Brown's paper and the present day, another librarian, L. Stanley Jast, read a paper entitled 'Bibliography and the deluge: I accuse'.[1] A few sentences will indicate how close Jast was to Brown in his thinking.

'Of what then do I accuse bibliographers? I accuse them of shirking in the face of an ever-increasing, devastating deluge of printed matter, the duty of controlling the torrent – stemming it, alas, being beyond their power – and rendering first aid to drowning humanity. I accuse them of being bound, hand and foot, by the fetish of completeness . . . I accuse them of pottering in relatively unimportant back-waters. . . .

'In this respect much of modern bibliography, even when approximate completeness is not envisaged, amounts to little more than a census of paper spoiled by being printed on. What has been called the dream of bibliography is in reality a nightmare. Its accomplishment would add to the world's burden, not lighten it, for to record rubbish is only less a crime than to publish it.'

'It will', Jast hoped and dreamed 'be the primary aim of the new bibliography not to collect more titles but to sift them, not to record anything and everything but to eliminate the chaff from the grain, and to preserve the grain only. Complete bibliographies in the old sense will be regarded as bad bibliographies. . . .

[1] *Library Association Record*: Vol. 38 (1936). pp. 353-360.

'To take off the scum -- that should be the one object of bibliography, its alpha and omega. It is selective bibliography on the principle, not of inclusion but of exclusion.'

The need was identical in the opinions of both librarians and they were in forthright agreement that it was the bibliographers who were to blame. Similar criticisms can still be heard from time to time and it is obvious that bibliography can provide an easy target if its basic nature is not clearly understood. Pollard had insisted that the business of the bibliographer was primarily 'the enumeration of books', 'the lowly task of finding out what books exist, and thereby helping to secure their preservation.' The subject list, which presupposes evaluation of the contents and the exclusion of items, the graded literature guides and surveys, are essential tools but it is not within the competency of the bibliographer to provide them, unless he is an appropriate subject specialist as well. A bibliography must be uncritical in its approach so far as the subject matter is concerned and the comprehensive nature of a bibliography must be accepted if the word is to have any real meaning. In Greg's words, 'It is the end that the enumeration is to subserve that determines whether a work is bibliographical or not. If the enumeration is governed by the subject-matter of the books then it is not bibliographical. A bibliographer has no business to know a bible from a Decameron or a sermon from a fabliau. An enumeration of books of patristic theology or on the structure of the atom has no place in bibliographical science, in spite of the fact that it is traditionally and quite reasonably called a "bibliography".'[1]

Greg's opinion was that it was quite reasonable for some of these listings to be called 'bibliographies', yet probably, as the situation has deteriorated over the years, this is the crux of the problem. If no reliance can be placed on the correct, or pedantic according to some critics, use of the word then each has to be judged on the basis of a service which it did not set out to

---

[1] *The Library*: Fourth Series. Vol. XIII (1932–33). p. 253.

perform. In some cases the prefatory material alone provides a clue to the fact that the compiler had some kind of limitation in mind when he surveyed the field.

The usefulness of a selective or evaluative listing is also diminished by incorrect terminology. Any list, provided by one who is expert in the subject concerned, has a value entirely of its own and one which should not be confused with the uncritical, properly so-called bibliography. John Carter and John Sparrow's *A. E. Housman: an Annotated Hand-list* is strengthened by the fact that, since it did not intend to be a full dress bibliography, it did not call itself such but simply an 'unassuming hand-list'.[1] The situation is clarified at the outset and no user could claim to have been misled by the title. The compilers each enjoyed established reputations as Housman enthusiasts and scholars, consequently the hand-list had an authority which would not necessarily be overshadowed by a comprehensive bibliography. A bibliography and a hand-list serve different purposes; one is not a pale shadow of the other and each category has its own wide range of varied accomplishments. Similarly Michael Sadleir's *XIX Century Fiction* had the sub-title 'a bibliographical record based on his own collection'.[2] In the dedication of the work Sadleir referred to it as a catalogue. Under either nomenclature it was quite clear that it had no pretention to being a bibliography of nineteenth-century fiction or even of nineteenth-century fiction in English, or indeed of nineteenth-century English fiction. In both these examples, however, more is added than is taken away by this avoidance of a bibliography. Carter and Sparrow's judgements as to the importance of individual items in the cases of inclusion or exclusion in their hand-list are valuable. Michael Sadleir's compilation was based directly on the collection which he built up over a considerable period; a collection which reflected not

[1] *CARTER*, John and *SPARROW*, John. *A. E. Housman: an Annotated Hand-list*. 1952.
[2] *SADLEIR*, Michael. *XIX Century Fiction: a bibliographical record, based on the author's own collection*. 2 vols. 1951.

simply his personal interests but also his own particular bibliographical expertise.

No question at all arises of a bibliography's being in some curious way superior in status to a reading list, or literature guide, or even a select bibliography. Different purposes are served by these tools and the confusion would be less marked if care was observed regarding nomenclature.

It is, however, perfectly natural and frequently desirable to confine a bibliography within certain specific limitations. The important thing is that this limitation should be factual rather than critical. A 'bibliography' of Robert Louis Stevenson would contain references to all writings by him, irrespective of when or where they were published or in whatever language. If critical writings about him and his work were to be included, and this is normally required in the bibliographical survey of an author, then the same all-inclusiveness must prevail. So soon as any title is excluded as unimportant, then the critical factor enters in and the work loses status as a bibliography. Limitations must be applied, if any are necessary, which involve no critical judgement or, at least, only critical judgement of a bibliographical nature. Thus a bibliography of first editions of Stevenson is a feasible proposition or a bibliography restricted to prose works or poems. Equally a bibliography of his writings in English or his writings in translation are valid fields for purely bibliographical work. Chronological divisions are particularly appropriate, especially when they conform to important bibliographical or biographical patterns in the author's life and work. For example, the text of an author as evidenced in the editions published during his lifetime have a special importance in that they could incorporate authorial revisions. A bibliography can, therefore, be reasonably restricted to such printings. In all these examples the important point is that the limiting factor is not one which is liable to be affected by a purely subjective approach

Greg's view of this kind of bibliographical limitation was expressed in his paper in the Bibliographical Society's fiftieth anniversary volume. 'The enumeration, that is, either of all books or of some *bibliographically* defined subdivision, as for example clay cylinders (cuneiform), papyri (roll or codex), manuscripts (on paper or vellum), block-books, incunabula, "English books to 1640" (i.e. printed or sold in England), Aldines, illustrated books, and so on. I think that books written or printed in a particular script or type – uncial, Carolingian, secretary, roman, black-letter, Cyrillic – form bibliographical classes, but not books in a particular language. This does not mean that I depreciate "subject" bibliographies – after all, my own work has been mainly devoted to one – but only that, being governed (except in a case of a "bibliography of bibliography") by non-geographical considerations, I do not regard them as one of the tasks of bibliography.'[1]

There are many examples of factual and bibliographical limitations within the field of enumerative bibliography and their effectiveness can be judged by actual use. One of the outstanding examples of enumerative bibliography in modern times and one which has exerted considerable influence in so many varied areas of study is the *Short-title Catalogue* of Pollard and Redgrave.[2] Its success has been so marked that it has done much more than simply record the books of a period. It has given its name to the whole corpus of books of that age; an 'S.T.C. book' is a far more usual form of reference than 'an English book printed before 1640'. Ever since its inauguration in 1894, as is evidenced by the records of its early meetings, the Bibliographical Society had set, as one of its major objectives, the compilation of a bibliography of English literature. Some members saw this as the chief duty to be undertaken by the Society but, although it continued to be a subject for discussion for years, nothing positive ever resulted; at least, not in the direction as originally intended. When vague plans began to

---

[1] *Studies in Retrospect*. p. 25n.

[2] *POLLARD*, A. W. and *REDGRAVE*, G. R. *A Short-title Catalogue of books printed in England, Scotland and Ireland, and of English books printed abroad, 1475–1640*. 1926.

take on a most positive aspect, then the proposals appeared with a strict chronological limitation. On 21st January 1918 a paper prepared by A. W. Pollard was read at a meeting of the Bibliographical Society. Pollard's lectures were generally read for him by a friend because of the stammer from which he suffered throughout his life. On this occasion the Journal of the Society, printed in the *Transactions*, recorded the subject matter of the paper as ' "The Output of English Printing during the first twenty years after the grant of a Charter to the Stationers' Company", but better described as *Plans for Bibliographical Work on the Sixteenth Century*'.[1] Pollard admitted later that he wandered somewhat from his brief on that occasion but he did suggest that there was need for a 'short-title handlist' of early English books 'leaving a full-dress catalogue to be produced when we know enough to make it a good one'. One of Pollard's great and most marked characteristics was his wish to translate all schemes and projects for work into reality with as short a delay as possible. On this occasion he was helped by the fact that G. R. Redgrave, a Vice-President who took the chair for Pollard's paper, stated that he was prepared to make available a sum of money in order to help the project forward. A team of assistants, each with a specialized area of printing as his or her prime responsibility, began to gather around the joint editors. The British Museum, the Bodleian Library, and the Librarian of the Henry E. Huntington Library in California all gave direct assistance in a manner which ensured that those major collections should be fully represented.

The result of these labours, finally published in 1926, was a publication which, apart from its now proven uses, is a perfect example of an enumerative bibliography and exactly what such a work can accomplish. It left no doubt as to the precise scope of the bibliography. It was essentially 'a catalogue of the books of which its compilers have been able to locate copies, not a bibliography of books known or believed to have been pro-

[1] *Transactions of the Bibliographical Society*. Vol. XV (1917–1919) p. 5.

duced'. The dates of the period covered are definite and a clear statement was given as to the definition of 'English' books. The term was held to include 'all books in whatever language printed in England, Wales, Scotland and Ireland, and all books in English wherever printed, also Latin service-books, wherever printed, if for use in England and Scotland. It does not include works by English authors printed out of England in Latin or any language other than English.' The qualifications made here are important not only because they clarify the scope of the work beyond any doubt, but also they acknowledge the main facts of printing and publishing history of the time. It would, for example be highly anachronistic to expect to find any appreciable number of entries in the category of Latin service-books for dates much later than 1640, whereas for the S.T.C. period it is a vitally important corpus of printing as can be particularly judged by the fact that 'Liturgies' extend from 15790 to 16607 in the serial numbering. Even at the outset the S.T.C., in this way, demonstrates the fact that, although an enumerative bibliography can be described as the simplest form of bibliography, it is so in one sense only. Its simplicity lies in the fact that it has a perfectly clear-cut function and that, with bibliographical apparatus stripped down to an absolute minimum, it is easy to use and understand. Its ease in use is not, however, necessarily matched by a similar ease in compilation. The S.T.C. has enjoyed an almost unrivalled reputation for forty years because of the rigid standards of scholarship which its compilers brought to the task. The new S.T.C., for which the editorial work was largely undertaken by F. S. Ferguson and W. A. Jackson and which, after both their deaths, is expected to complete about 1970, will be in many respects a direct result of the success of the original work. The original S.T.C. stimulated bibliographical work in the period to such an extent that a high percentage of 'unrecorded' titles will appear in the new work. This is a frequent, and highly important, by-product of a good bibliography. It is not the finish to an area of study but rather a tool which is produced so that study may begin.

49

It would be difficult, and indeed fundamentally undesirable, to attempt to lay down any hard and fast regulations as to the exact shape and content of an entry in an enumerative bibliography. For efficient use the entries must vary according to the particular type of material which is being listed. The S.T.C. is, nevertheless, such a good example of this category that an entry can be looked at in more detail to provide some indication as to the chief elements which will be regarded as necessary.

Two extremely famous books came within the scope of the S.T.C. and provide useful bases for discussion because entries of various kinds can be found for them both in many other classes of bibliography.

> 2216. The holy bible, conteyning the old testament and the new: newly translated out of the originall tongues. Appointed to be read in churches. [Royal version. Ruth iii, 15 'he went'.] fol. *R. Barker*, 1611. L.O.C. HH.; HN. N. NY.

In the S.T.C. this entry occupies five lines; yet within that space a large amount of purely factual information has been concentrated. To begin with the work now has an internationally recognized form of reference in its serial number. In the case of some publications this is of only minimal importance but in this instance the particular advantages can easily be seen. Entries for the 'Bible' in the S.T.C. extend from numbers 2055 to 3046 inclusive. Although entries under the various sub-headings such as 'Bible-English' are arranged chronologically, precise identification, without reference to a serial number, can occasionally be difficult because of the mass of material gathered here in close proximity. The title is set out in sufficient detail for identification and the format, printer and date duly listed. Over and above this, the particular issue under question is specified by the variant reading in one verse and the revised text shown in similar fashion in the entry for the second edition in entry number 2217.

The other feature of the entry is one which is not common to all bibliographies of whatever category but whose usefulness cannot be denied. The more uncommon the material the more important it becomes that some information regarding the location of copies should be given. The editors made it clear in their preface that their original intention was that there 'should be three for those in English ownership and two for copies in the United States'. Initial reactions to the news of publication, and above all the offer of Messrs. Quaritch to put an edition on sale of the same size as that for the members of the Society, allowed for a change of plan; '. . . now in the case of books of special interest, such as plays, reference to as many as five or six English and five or six American examples were sometimes admitted. Users of the book must, however, again be warned that it has not been compiled as a census of copies, but only to inform students where copies can most conveniently be consulted. Thus when a book is in the British Museum the existence of other copies at Lambeth Palace and Sion College is not generally mentioned; again, when a book is not in the British Museum or the Bodleian or the University Library, Cambridge, then copies in other libraries in London, Oxford and Cambridge are mentioned, if known. Thus it is only when less than three copies are recorded from English sources, and less than two from libraries in the United States, that any deduction can be drawn that the copies mentioned are all of which the compilers had notes.' Against this background of policy a considerable amount of detail can be established regarding the accessibility of copies.

The other example is of an equally famous entry.

22273. SHAKESPEARE, WILLIAM. Mr. William Shakespeares comedies, histories, & tragedies. Published according to the true originall copies. fol. *Printed by Isaac Iaggard, and Ed. Blount.* 1623. Colophon; *Printed at the charges of W. Iaggard, Ed. Blount, I. Smithweeke, and W. Aspley,* 1623. Ent. 8 no. L. (5 copies, one w. portrait in first state), O (2 copies, one as delivered by Stat. Co.), C, DUR³. M; HN. Folger (numerous copies), N. NY. WH. *See* Sir S. Lee's Census, etc.

Here the main essentials are as for the 1611 Bible. In addition, there is the transcription of the colophon; the note of entry in the Stationers' Company Register; fuller detail regarding the location of copies; and a reference to a larger census. With an entry of twelve lines this constitutes probably the longest entry for any book in the S.T.C. The amount of information contained within this limited space, while remarkable in its compression, is only a small fraction of the quantity of detailed bibliographical facts which are relevant to the study of this particular work. The succintness of the entry in an enumerative bibliography is occasioned not by the fact that it is the limit of the bibliographical information which is of real interest, but rather because the purpose of the listing demands a brief, concise entry. This can best be shown by comparing the two entries mentioned with the fuller entry in the catalogue of the British and Foreign Bible Society in the first case and, in the second, with the entry in Greg's *Bibliography of the English Printed Drama to the Restoration*.[1] In both instances the entry is considerably more detailed and in the case of the first Folio it is an extremely full description covering some four pages for the work as a whole and additional entries for each individual play.

Another example of an enumerative bibliography which includes a large quantity of compressed material for all the entries throughout its wide range is the *World List of Scientific Periodicals*.[2] The type of material listed is totally unlike that in the S.T.C. and, consequently, requires a different kind of entry. On the whole the material is recent and for the most part of little purely bibliographical interest. The problem is once again that of listing, with the basically important details, a vast amount of material; in the fourth edition over sixty thousand titles are recorded.

[1] British and Foreign Bible Society. Library. *Historical catalogue of the printed editions of Holy Scripture in the library of the . . . Society*. 2 vols in 4. 1903–1911.

GREG, W. W. *A Bibliography of the English Printed Drama to the Restoration.* 4 vols. 1939–1959.

[2] *World List of Scientific Periodicals* published in the years 1900–1960. 4th ed. by Peter Brown and George Burder Stratton. 3 vols. 1963–1965.

Compared with the S.T.C., the *World List* raises a number of fresh problems. In the 'Editors' Note' a statement is made as to the exact scope of the list. 'This present edition is of exactly the same pattern as the previous editions, but now covering the period 1900 to 1960. It includes periodicals concerned with the natural sciences and technology of which issues were published during this period of sixty-one years. Periodicals first published at any time before 1900 are listed so long as they continued publication into the twentieth century; changes of title taking place before 1900 are not shown. At the other end of the period a change of title taking place after 1960 is noted, but no separate entries have been made for the post-1960 titles ... some ten thousand titles which appeared in the third edition have been excluded from the present edition as being of social or commercial interest rather than scientific. The period 1951 to 1960 was one of greatly increased publication of scientific and technological periodicals, with the result that entries for periodicals published during these ten years account for about a quarter of this present edition of the *World List*.'

The field is here clearly delimited and the very terms which might appear to need careful definition ('periodical'; 'natural sciences' and 'technology') are not over difficult of understanding. No question of critical evaluation of the material in the strictest sense arises apart from the exclusion of titles which have 'social or commercial interest rather than scientific'. This limitation is, however, exercised more on the grounds of appropriateness within the definition rather than quality.

The individual entry for the title covers precisely the same ground as the S.T.C., giving serial number, title, detail of publication and location. Additional material, necessitated by the specialized nature of the works listed, includes a recognized abbreviated form of the periodical's title. For the reader meeting a title such as *Botanicheskie materialy Gerbariya Glavnago botanicheskago sada*, it is a relief to know that the world will recognize the periodical of this title under the abbreviation 'Bot mater. Gerb. glavn. bot. Sada'. Detail of imprint is usually restricted, compared with the usage of the S.T.C., to the place of publication. A typical entry reads as follows:

> 13489. Ceiba. A scientific journal issued by the Escuela agricola panamerica. Tegucigalpa. Ceiba. [1950] L. bm^n; HS; K; TP 62 – (English ed.); Y.

The location index is based on a comparatively small list of British libraries of some seventy-five in London and in some sixty-five provincial centres.

In each of these examples it is apparent that the compilers have avoided the use of the term 'bibliography'. One is a 'Catalogue' and one is a 'List'. This nomenclature is based primarily on the element of the 'finding tool' or 'location list' in each case. Although they are totally different publications in regard to the materials which they list, they have much in common. Early English printed books, on the one hand, of which the chief interest in a high percentage of cases is historical and bibliographical; on the other hand, periodicals in many different languages where the interest lies almost completely in the subject matter; yet these have forms of entry which are almost identical. The similarity is brought about by the fact that enumeration of items seldom goes far enough to reveal the differences of a purely bibliographical nature. If bibliographical description were carried to further levels it is unlikely that a Polish periodical on inorganic chemistry in the 1920's would have much in common with Michael Drayton's *Ideas Mirrour* of 1594.

One of the great benefits of both the S.T.C. and the W.L.S.P. has been their location listings and with experience of such tools it becomes difficult to imagine a bibliography of this scale in the future which did not include locations of copies. This being so, another type of highly specialized location list is of importance in this field; the published catalogues of libraries. Although a catalogue of a library can never be a bibliography in the strict sense of the word, it can fulfil certain conditions which will make it of outstanding importance as a bibliographical tool. The main requirements are that:

(i) the collection which is recorded is itself of particular merit, and

(ii) the catalogue is good in itself.

The collection may either be a general one of considerable depth or a more specialized one with a narrow subject field of interest. Naturally, the great National Libraries of the world provide good examples of the general repertory of books and the importance of such collections may be judged from the catalogues of the British Museum (London), the Library of Congress (Washington) and the Bibliothèque Nationale (Paris). It is to be expected that the major specialization in each case will be in the respective national literatures and this is so, but it is very far from being to the exclusion of major holdings in other fields. It is difficult to make any valid comparison of the respective strengths of holdings in catalogues which represent different dates of completion for each entry. Nevertheless, using the three catalogues already mentioned as examples, interesting relationships can be established by comparing the holdings of each library in, say, Dickens, Emerson and Hugo. The pre-eminence of the national collection is apparent but the standing and importance of the other two cannot be denied.

All analyses, as well as the sterner test of actual use, would confirm the outstanding importance of each library. Each library would, at the same time, readily acknowledge the small proportion quantitively of the world's published output in its holdings. In spite of the levelling effects on national holdings of schemes of legal deposit of books, each library has operated a policy of selectivity over the years, if only because it was forced by financial stringency. Thus the percentage of important material is very much more substantial than the percentage of actual material and each catalogue has its foundations in sub-ject selectivity on a non-bibliographical basis. This aspect of the catalogues, combined with the fact that they constitute 'one-place' location lists, will always cause them to rank very highly in general usefulness. The part which a great National Library catalogue can play as a major bibliographical tool is exemplified by the position occupied in British bibliography by the general author catalogue of the British Museum. The printing of the catalogue was a matter of major discussion in the Museum on many separate occasions during the first half of the nineteenth century. By the middle of the century it had progressed no further than what, in Esdaile's words, was 'the fiasco of the 1841 Catalogue'. As the publication plans began to assume a more definite shape after the turn of the mid-century, there were already several interested observers who saw the value of the catalogue as a general bibliographical tool. Charles Wentworth Dilke raised considerable hopes, and also opposition, when he began to develop his suggestions along these lines. He attracted many notable supporters such as Sir Henry Cole but he had a majority of uninterested observers.

There were those few who saw the catalogue not simply as an important bibliographical tool but also one which served a wider purpose and contributed towards the solution of an age-old problem. When Richard Garnett was enlisting support for the publication of the British Museum Catalogue in 1882, he wrote, '. . . to support the Museum Catalogue is to take a long step towards the attainment of the still grander object of a Universal Catalogue. At present a Universal Catalogue is a Utopian Catalogue. I have the greatest respect for those who have advocated it as an undertaking immediately practicable. I have no doubt that the twentieth century will speak of them as men before their age. But they *are* before it. Their project is at present intricate, intangible. They want a base of operations . . . this Catalogue supplies such a base.'[1]

The other major role which can be fulfilled by a published catalogue operating as a bibliographical tool is when it is of a specialized collection. Many examples can be found of printed catalogues of specialist collections which become established as pieces of major bibliographical apparatus. Again, one example will serve to indicate the purpose of such tools. One of the

[1] Conference Proceedings of the 5th Annual Conference of the Library Association.

major general 'bibliographies' in the social sciences is *A London Bibliography of the Social Sciences*,[1] Its title makes it clear beyond all doubt that it was conceived as a bibliography, yet its sub-title goes on to elaborate it as 'the subject catalogue of'nine libraries, the most important of which was the British Library of Political and Economic Science. Essentially a catalogue leading into major specialist collections, it nevertheless never loses sight of its purely bibliographical role. The bibliographical descriptions of the titles listed are very brief, as is consistent with the purpose of this type of catalogue, yet a bibliography in a book is noted. Similarly, in another field, the major bibliographies of the Bible are the catalogue of the library of the British and Foreign Bible Society and the volumes covering the 'Bible' in the main catalogue of the British Museum.

In all such instances of printed catalogues being used as bibliographical tools, whether of large general or specialized libraries, the quality of the collection is the prime consideration. The second main requirement is that the publication should be technically competent considered simply as a catalogue. Although revolution is in the air in cataloguing, as will soon be discussed, it is a change which is only now, and slowly, beginning to have any profound effect on printed and published catalogues. All areas of bibliographical work, however, from the simplest cataloguing through enumerative bibliography and on to the most advanced areas of descriptive bibliography have been subjected to vitally important new influences during the past twenty years or so which are having far reaching effects on the efficiency of the products. Modern methods and standards of analytical bibliography are producing descriptive bibliographies of steadily advancing sophistication and range. Similarly, fresh techniques and improved methods are changing enumerative bibliography in a way which becomes clear when the more traditional methods of bibliography compilation are viewed in all their settled pattern.

[1] *London Bibliography of the Social Sciences.* 4 vols. 1931–32 ; suppl. 7 vols. 1934–1960.

For a variety of purposes and for a whole range of bibliographical publications the general principles of enumerative
bibliography have long been accepted and virtually unchal-
lenged. If one accepts the role of the library catalogue as a part
of this overall pattern, there is no reason to reject Gaselee's
suggestion that the Alexandrian library produced the first real
example in the field. Its bibliographical interest, although very
real, was, nevertheless, almost an accidental side-issue. There
is no doubt that its primary function was to serve as a catalogue
to the one collection. For many centuries this was to remain as
true a reason for the compilation of similar lists as it is today for
the great research libraries. Occasionally, a utilitarian and
frankly didactic purpose was the motivation for many of the
early lists rather than a disinterested bibliographical usage. St
Jerome's *De Scriptoribus Ecclesiasticis* which he compiled around
420 was such a list and one which remained of sufficient importance to appear among early printed books in an Augsburg
edition of 1470. At the end of his eighth-century *Historia
Ecclesiastica Gentis Anglorum* the Venerable Bede added 'Notitia
de seipso et de libris suis', primarily as a listing of his own works.
As would be expected the fundamental change came with the
advent of the printed book. As the number of individual titles
grew and as multiplication of copies made access to the works
much easier and more widespread, so the need for more comprehensive listings, especially within subject fields, became
necessary.

The work which could well make claim to be the earliest
'pure' enumerative bibliography was the *Liber de Scriptoribus
Ecclesiasticis* of Johann Tritheim printed by Amerbach in Basle
in 1494. It is 'pure' in the sense that it was produced specifically as a bibliographical list and not with any secondary purpose. Lists in other subject fields followed over the years,
notably in theology, law and medicine. In the early years of the
sixteenth century the role of such lists would seem to have been
clearly established. The fact that such a wide variety of publishers and printers were prepared to publish them provides at

least some indication that they enjoyed a measure of financial success and public regard.

Throughout the sixteenth, seventeenth and eighteenth centuries listings proliferated. Many were national or subject bibliographies and this produced a naturally imposed limitation on the size and complexity of the lists. From the seventeenth century onwards, trade lists were slow in establishing themselves on any sizeable scale and, in any event, the total amount of any country's book production was sufficiently modest not to raise any of those problems which result from having to deal with large quantities of material. Compared with the overwhelming bulk of many libraries of the present day their predecessors up to and including the greater part of the nineteenth century were comparatively small. Books had not yet grown out of hand and the problem of the periodical was hardly as yet a cloud on the horizon. From whatever date we wish to place the beginnings of bibliographical work, whether in the Alexandrian library or later, there was a long history of enumerative bibliography until the nineteenth century during which no special problems were encountered. The basic principles remained fundamentally the same and no especial consideration was given to any aspects of bibliographical compilation. There was a clearly defined task to be accomplished and lists of all kinds flowed without respite.

The nineteenth century changed all that. The mechanization of all the parts of the book industry during that century brought about changes more revolutionary than anything which had happened since the time of Gutenberg. In retrospect we can see clearly that during the period from 1800 to 1900 there was absolutely no part of the book trade which was not vitally affected. Very many different claims have been produced for the importance of the various parts of this revolution, but as time goes by we can see with increasing clarity the over-riding importance of the sheer quantitative advance in the productive capacity of the printing press. This feature had a lasting effect on much more than the book trade itself.

Iwinski calculated that world book production doubled between 1858 and 1898 and, additionally, that the number of periodicals nearly quadrupled from 1866 to 1898. This latter circumstance raised an entirely fresh problem. Until this time the majority of periodicals had been, if not ephemeral publications, at least primary repositories of general literature. The situation changed as an increasing number of specialist periodicals began publication. Without consideration of these there were many subjects, and particularly scientific and technical ones, of which the full bibliography would be very incomplete. The now somewhat forgotten figure of Frank Campbell of the British Museum was one of the most insistent of those who demanded that the bibliography of a country, an author, a period or a subject should be really complete.

So soon as this idea is grasped then another key factor came into consideration. To a greater extent than most books a periodical is a conglomeration of individual items. Although a basic unity can be traced in these in many specialized subject periodicals, they are not infrequently quite disparate. Traditionally a bibliography was likely to be considered as a listing of books, or, occasionally, a listing of periodicals. It rapidly became apparent, however, that in many instances a bibliography, certainly in the terms in which Campbell conceived it, would need to be an enumeration of individual items. Some of these would be books, some periodicals; many would be separate items from periodicals. One of the most significant changes in bibliographical compilation of the last half century has been the increasing weight given to this kind of analytical entry. It is not simply in the scientific and technical fields that this is of prime importance. To take one example from literature. The two best known bibliographies of Shakespeare, those by Jaggard and by Ebisch and Schücking, are primarily records of published books. Yet a bibliography of Shakespeare which ignores the vast amount of material which has appeared in periodicals and learned journals is a very incomplete affair.

The realization has been growing more and more insistently

in recent years and as the total amount of book and periodical publication has increased, so has the demand for more specific information grown alongside. Now the position has reached truly alarming proportions. We have passed through the stage, to which Campbell's work bears witness, of realizing that many a bibliography is incomplete unless it includes analytical material from periodicals. Now we have reached the stage at which we realize that this is not sufficient. An article in a periodical, a separate treatise in a book, each is in itself a collection of individual items of 'thought units'. If a bibliography is to be of maximum value it must enumerate all these isolated pieces of information which are frequently of prime importance. In any event, as Pollard and Campbell both suggested, it is for the subject specialist to make any necessary selection not the bibliographer. This is an area in which the world of the librarian and the world of the bibliographer have moved very close in recent years. The enumerative bibliographer is concerned to be able to list all the specific references to a subject just as the librarian is anxious to use the results. We must, consequently, expect that this one area of enumerative bibliography at least will be required to advance in new directions.

In March 1964, the Council on Library Resources published a report which had been prepared for it entitled, 'Toward the Library of the 21st Century'. This report started off with the words, 'We do not know what the library of the future will look like or how it will work. We do know, however, that the world's store of literature now amounts to hundreds of millions of different books, and in the next century will reach billions.

'We also know that sheer numbers cannot measure the entire burden of seeking and using information needed in the carrying out of intellectual pursuits, such as those in research, especially when those pursuits draw upon knowledge that obsolesces almost as fast as it is gained.'

The figures which the Report produced were of a world store of printed matter now standing at 200 million different books and doubling every fifteen to twenty years. It is the size of the problem, from the viewpoint of enumeration, which raises the most fundemental issues.

Overwhelming, however, as this problem seems to be, every librarian and research worker knows that there is a still larger one just concealed. In a large number of inquiries a reader is not concerned with the whole of the book but with certain specific pieces of information. In many instances the inquirer does not even require to see the book itself provided he can be fed with his succinct answers. For the kind of reference work which is embodied in this idea an index is a vital part of the book, practically as vital as the text itself. If a book is adequately indexed then the reader knows that each piece of information or thought unit can easily be recovered. Since it is these thought units, rather than the whole of the somewhat artificial unity of the book, which are ultimately the objects of the search then it is still these which are of paramount importance in a collection of books as in a single volume. As an index to a book provides the exact kind of enumeration required, so a vast cumulation of perfect indexes to all recorded materials could give that kind of control for which bibliographers have always sought.

This, then, after centuries in which affairs ran in a reasonably controlled fashion, has been the crux of the problem of the past hundred years. An immense advance in the amount of material produced has been followed by an increasingly intense specialization in demand. The realization of what has been happening has been gradual and, consequently, the remedies proposed for the solution of the problem have evolved gradually in an attempt to meet a changing stiuation.

The nineteenth century saw, chiefly in Germany and France, the vast increase in the number of retrospective bibliographies in special subject fields. This was the first and most basically important step towards the organization of the material leading towards a more specific reference. Along the same lines the century produced the first specialized periodical bibliographies in major subject fields. Any glance at the range of bibliographic tools from the early years of the century on will demonstrate how seriously the problem was taken. The main directions in which the efforts were made equally suggest an awareness of the problem. As these retrospective bibliographies grew and as they were matched with current and trade bibliographies the overall chronological coverage improved rapidly. Yet the knowledge of the demand for an increased specificity of approach did not lead bibliographers to forget the years-old dream of the universal bibliography.

It was a Parisian bookseller, Charles Jacques Brunet, who was responsible for one of the most famous of all the universal bibliographies on a selective basis. It typifies more completely than any other work the type of need which the century saw for this kind of work. Brunet's first edition of his *Manuel du Libraire* was issued in 1810, when he was thirty years of age. For the next fifty years it remained Brunet's chief preoccupation and it was enlarged quite significantly with each issue. The fifth edition in six volumes of 1860–1865 is the one which had by far the widest circulation and by which he is now best remembered. He had calculated that the 30,000 titles included in his fourth edition represented less than a thirteenth of the total number of books printed. He was, consequently, very conscious of the fact that he had been selective and however subjective his choice had been he was fully aware of the basis on which it was made. He set himself the task of describing 'old books which are both rare and precious and a great number of modern books which by their widely recognized merit, their singularity, the beauty of their production, the illustrations with which they are ornamented, or by some other peculiarity may be ranked among the valuable books'. These descriptions were detailed and, in the light of the knowledge of the period, accurate. They were charmingly discursive and enlivened on a number of occasions with Brunet's own not-inconsiderable humour. It was a bibliography which carried into the period of our increasingly necessary expertise some at least of the best traditions of the old-style bookseller-bibliographer. Brunet remained readable in the same sense that Dibdin had been readable, but with a vastly greater sense of accuracy and knowledge of bibliography.

Up to the end of the first three-quarters of the nineteenth century nobody could complain that this period did not tackle the problems of which it was aware and went some way along the road to their solution. Brunet's work also advanced his suggestion for what was, by this time, coming to be regarded as a remaining fundamental problem – that of ordering the arrangement of the material. Brunet produced a classified index to his book which was an attempt to produce an arrangement which would help to organize his material advantageously. It was not an entirely new venture from every point of view since he relied and built upon the several previously published schemes and especially that of Prosper Marchand of 1706. Although it was widely used during the nineteenth century, particularly by booksellers, it cannot now be regarded as one which had any great impact upon the theory of classification. Nevertheless, followed as it was by series of classification schemes which had as their primary purpose the organization of materials in libraries, it stands as one great example of the 'bookstore system' and as evidence that the mid-part of the last century was fully apprised of the difficulty.

The years of enumerative bibliography since Brunet have been in large part concerned with the problem of the organization of the material. An individual bibliography or bibliographical tool, especially those of a publishable nature, has a problem of arrangement which, although important, is quite different in character. Increasingly as each year goes by, the idea of enumerative bibliography and the idea of universal bibliography must become more closely associated. The need for such bibliographical control is of ever-increasing importance and it is only within the rather limited and precise terminology of what has always been called enumerative or systematic bibliography that it is ever likely to be achieved; at least, within the measurable future. It will also serve to answer the most fundamental bibliographical question of all; what material exists? It is a later and more detailed search to discover the true nature of such material and some realization as to how it might be utilized. But first things must come first.

The modern world of enumerative bibliography, with a full realization of the problems, the requirements and the germ of a solution, began in 1895. This was the year of the foundation of the International Institute of Bibliography in Brussels. It was financed by the Belgian Government but, in all other respects, it was the achievement of two men. Paul Otlet and Henri Lafontaine were both Belgian lawyers. Their dream was of a great international index on cards listing everything printed since the beginning of European printing, irrespective of country of origin, language or subject, It would comprise an author list and a classified catalogue. They saw it as an enterprise which would flourish by international agreement among co-operating countries and could begin to bring some measure of standardization to the extremely variable biblio-graphical practices of various countries.

Paul Otlet, who was the leading figure in the enterprise, made a two-pronged initial approach to the problem. In the space of five years or so, he gathered together catalogues of libraries and institutions, bibliographies, booksellers' catalogues and any other likely source, cut them up, mounted them on cards and so produced seventeen million cards of his basic reference bibliography. He adapted and expanded the Decimal Classification scheme of Melvil Dewey and so launched the Universal Decimal Classification. This was the initial attempt to deal with the two problems – the collection of the references themselves and their organization.

Otlet's dream was important even though, in his lifetime, he could do no more than glimpse the possiblity of its ultimate fulfilment. The years until the beginning of the Second World War were a period during which much thought was given to the issues which he raised. The work of the International Federation of Documentation proceeded steadily and many half-forgotten individuals, such as S. C. Bradford, devoted considerable attention to the problems. The idea of documentation took shape even though, up to the present, nobody has succeeded in defining it with accuracy and clarity. In essence, it sets out to do the work which enumerative bibliography had tackled for so long and called new tools to its aid. This is, indeed, the factor which has changed the whole approach to this area of bibliographical work than any other.

Yet another new approach to the matter has taken shape since 1945. The old idea, never completely abandoned since the days of Gesner, was revived in a more practical form. The thought developed that universal bibliographical coverage could be achieved by bringing together national bibliographies throughout the world. Many of these were already in print, many of them already had, or planned to have, good programmes for achieving current coverage. Many revolved around the major collections of national libraries where great printed catalogues themselves provided a bibliographical bedrock. The survey, sponsored by Unesco and carried out by the Library of Congress, urged something along these lines when its report was issued in the early post-war years.[1] Since the time of the report the overall coverage has improved steadily. Because the majority of these tools were available in printed form another basic difficulty has been, at least, partially solved. Some of the early discussions on the creation of a universal bibliography in a universal documentation centre had failed to produce an answer as to the form and geographical disposition of the catalogue. Now that problem need exist no longer. It was not difficult to envisage that, as national coverage improved, universal coverage would not only improve but also that, in this form, it would have the capability of almost infinite multiplication. At the same time, however, as a breakthrough seemed possible in this area, it began to be realized that a quite distinct factor might well prove to be the most significant obstacle.

The crisis which now lies ahead of enumerative bibliography is clear and some consideration has been given to its solution

[1] Unesco/Library of Congress Bibliographical Survey. *Bibliographical Services, their present state and possibilities.* 1950.

even though nothing can yet be said positively to have emerged. If, as has been stressed, a bibliography cannot be 'selective', but limited only by factual considerations, then the time may well come when the output of literature is so vast that there is a dearth of useful limiting factors which can be applied.

This has been specifically isolated as a problem since the end of the last century. Even before that time individual scholars, like the Preacher, were lamenting the vast outpouring of books, but now the trickle has become a flood. Nobody worried more about this problem in the latter part of the nineteenth century than those librarians and scholars who were concerned, in some way or another, with the concept of a national or universal bibliography or catalogue. A few years after Richard Garnett had urged his idea of the acceptance of the British Museum Catalogue as a basis for a Universal Catalogue he spoke again of 'the growing perception of the difficulty of the undertaking'.

The increasing realization of the need for such a compilation, or at the very least for a really first-rate National Bibliography, coincided with a marked increase in the totals of books produced.

The more specific form of reference to the increasing output of pieces of information remains the particular problem. The concept of the national bibliography, even in the post-war years, has been primarily centred on the book as the unit. The book, in the sense that it is itself a collection of specific points of reference, other than in the instances such as dictionaries, or mathematical tables, for example, is seldom approached. If any analysis is done then it is usually of broad categories such as articles in periodicals rather than to the individual pieces of information. Yet in practically every branch of activity it is the unit of information which is required rather than the collection and it is of such units that adequate enumeration is needed.

Hitherto any such suggestion could only be greeted with sceptical laughter, but now modern scientific and technological developments are making this ideal more likely of achievement. Only something of the nature of a computer can hope to provide such a service but there is no longer any reason to doubt general practicability. The Council on Library Resources estimated that the number of bits, or binary digits, of information which would be contained by the world's total store of literature by the year 2000 would be 10,000,000,000,000,000, while the capacity of a fast random-access memory by the same date would be 10,000,000,000,000. It was, however, expected that the capacity of the memory would increase much more rapidly than that of the store of literature.

If this ever becomes a reality then the bibliographer will be within sight of one of his oldest objectives. Ever since the 'simple' listing and the basic cataloguing of books began, the wish has been for a basic record of the published material. This has been the role of enumerative bibliography; not to describe nor to evaluate, but to enumerate. Now that it is the thought-unit which we are trying to isolate the same overall methods will prevail but with modern and specially designed equipment.

Although much experimentation on these lines has been conducted in the post-war years, it is only recently that any clear indication of the kind of break-through which may soon be possible on a larger scale has been apparent. A large part of the work of enumerative bibliography consists of a painstaking and conscientious routine. It is precisely the type of operation which lends itself to the mechanistic approach. A not dissimilar approach is necessary for the compilation of concordances and the comparatively small number of first class concordances either on the market or on the shelves underlines the difficulties and the unattractiveness of this particular task. Within the last few years we have seen the first successful published concordances which were computer based. They have opened up completely new prospects in this area and this augurs well for the application of the same principle to enumerative bibliography. Harvard University Library, in 1965, produced the first computer based and printed section of its catalogue covering the Crusades. This is another step closer to the real needs of enumerative bibliography and makes full success by so much the more likely.

For centuries enumerative bibliography attempted to list books and references, either in general or in certain clear and specific areas. The problems have always been apparent and, as can be seen, notable attempts have been made to overcome them. Now, there is very real hope that an answer may be forthcoming.

3
Analytical
or
critical bibliography

If, as has been suggested, bibliography is the study of books as material objects then it follows logically that the first step in any bibliographical project is to subject the book to a purely physical examination. This can be conducted in many different ways for a variety of purposes, some of which may be appropriate to the function of bibliography and others may not. A book can, for example, and very frequently is, studied as a tangible object solely from the standpoint of the book arts or from its efficiency as a tool for conveying the message. In these instances, considerations of aesthetics will be paramount. They are legitimate and important areas of investigation but they are not a part of bibliography. There are other areas of study which are most open to doubt and can be regarded as peripheral to the main field as Greg did in his 1912 paper. 'Naturally enough the subject tends to shade off into others that are not bibliographical. Bookbinding is certainly a province of bibliography, yet it almost merges into a fine art, as do even more clearly book-illustration and illumination. Bibliography has to take cognizance of these subjects, but it can never make them altogether its own. Book-plates have a purely superficial connection with books: their study is but a bastard branch of the subject. Another useful limitation lies in this, that bibliography only concerns itself with processes that leave their mark on the character of the finished book. Printing it is very largely concerned with, but it does not study the mechanism of the modern steam press. Pens it is certainly interested in, but hardly in their growth or manufacture. It attends to the preparation of vellum, though indifferent to the breeding of calves.'[1]

The examination for bibliographical purposes is designed to discover all that can be discovered about the various procedures which go into the making of the whole book. This means that the series of actions through which the book will have passed have to be analysed in the terms of the effect which they had upon the finished production. These are the physical aspects which are of importance; anything which might be regarded as an analysis of a purely aesthetic nature is not of account. It will follow from this that one fruitful method of examination will follow the stages in the production of the books themselves. In all instances one basic principle may be observed: if each step in the production process were perfectly accomplished and therefore a perfect book resulted, there would be virtually no bibliographical problems at all. Assume that an author was able to prepare a clean readable manuscript of his work with all revisions included prior to its going to press. Assume that the compositor succeeded in translating that manuscript without error into composed type and that the printing process was accomplished without any kind of mistake. Assume that the sheets were correctly gathered and bound and that the finished product suffered no damage from the moment of publication until the present day. Assume that any subsequent printings of the work appeared in a similar miraculous manner free from any kind of taint or imperfection. In such cases bibliographical problems would disappear because there would be no difference between the work as it eventually appeared and as we hold it now and the form in which it was the author's and printer's intention that it should appear. Such a long and vital list of perfections has, in fact, probably never happened in the history of book production – or, at least, only in an extreme minority of cases. Bibliography, therefore, rests a major part of its case in

[1] *Transactions of the Bibliographical Society.* Vol. XII (1914) pp. 39–53.

imperfections and critical bibliography is very largely the examination of the book in order to discover in what ways it differs from the 'ideal copy', once this has been established.

This latter phrase is of fairly recent usage and is largely the creation of Fredson Bowers. By the use of this expression it is intended to convey full information regarding 'the actual most perfect form of the book achieved by the printer within an issue'.[1] This, naturally, comes to be of major importance in a bibliographical description which is being produced for a bibliography rather than a catalogue. The processes of analytical bibliography are in essence two-fold; one, through examination of multiple copies of an issue to establish the description, including the formulary of collation, of the ideal copy and, two to discover the difference between that and any individual copy. It will also be appreciated that the ideal copy may not be represented by any extant copy. Ideal copy is not concerned with matters governing the correctness of the text, or freedom from misprints, but simply with an assessment of the physical details of the book and their exact relationship to the state in which the book was planned to appear at the time of its initial publication. Every known copy of an issue of a book may well exhibit differences, of greater or less importance, from the state in which it was originally intended to appear.

A simple example will serve, at this point, to illustrate the kind of reasoning which the bibliographer may need to apply. Many printings of numerous works are represented by no more than one extant copy. It is far from uncommon for that unique copy to be imperfect. The examination of the book may reveal precisely what the imperfection is and some deductions may be made even though of a very limited nature. A missing leaf can be deduced from the knowledge of the bibliographical nature of the sheet and the structure of the gathering, but such a deduction cannot always indicate the nature of the leaf except in the broadest possible terms. Even the supposition that the missing

---

[1] For the fullest discussion on *ideal copy* see: *BOWERS*, Fredson. *Principles of Bibliographical Description*. 1949. (Re-issue, 1962).

leaf is probably a title-leaf, half-title-leaf or leaf of text will remain an unsupported theory so long as the uniqueness of the copy remains.

So soon as a second copy can be collated against another, then far more important conclusions may be reached. If the comparison of copies suggests the strong probability that they are both of the same issue, then the nature of the imperfections in the one copy can be deduced from the other. This may be so without any suggestion that the copies would be *identical* in any part.

For example, there are two recorded copies of Caxton's 1485 printing of Malory. That in the John Rylands Library, Manchester, is imperfect – wanting eleven leaves; the other, in the Pierpont Morgan Library, New York, is perfect. A comparison of the two copies makes it clear that they are not identical because important differences are found in areas where they cover common ground. There are thirty-three variants spread throughout the whole of the book but, in addition, 172 variants which are concentrated in the third sheet of gatherings N and Y which were thoroughly revised. Even so, the general collation of the two copies leaves no doubt that they were of the same issue. Since the general layout of variants throughout the book is established it is possible to hazard an intelligent opinion as to the closeness of the Morgan text to that on one of the missing Rylands' leaves. Such a comparison between two copies can, obviously permit more conclusions to be drawn than was possible from one isolated copy.

The discovery in 1945 of an early manuscript of Malory brought to light important new evidence and had a profound effect on the establishment of the text, but any future emergence of a third copy of the first printed version could radically change our attitudes regarding the nearness of the text in the case of the imperfect parts. Obviously the basic bibliographical task in relation to Caxton's *Malory* is to ascertain the relationship between the manuscript and this first printed text and also the ways in which each extant copy differs from the ideal and, consequently, from each other. This is the kind of situation which can arise when the total amount of available evidence is small and when, therefore, any new evidence adds an appreciable percentage increase.

In critical bibliography certain parts of the book and particular processes within the production of the book have come to be the most fruitful for analysis. Modern work in critical bibliography can serve to highlight these areas of research and to indicate the variety of problems which will be encountered.

The actual process of the examination of a book for bibliographical purposes is fairly generally called the collating of the work. It used to be said that this process of collation set out to answer three basic questions:

(a)   what work is this in hand,
(b)   which particular edition, version, recension, printing of the work is it,
(c)   is it complete and perfect or imperfect or made perfect?

As the first general guiding lines as to what it is important to discover these questions remain valid. The change which has occurred in thinking about them in recent years is the detail to which these questions may now, and frequently need to be, pursued. If twentieth-century bibliographical work can be said to have produced one outstanding reaction it is an appreciation of the importance of the individuality of the copy. At the time when the three questions were formulated and chiefly current it was widely considered to be sufficient to produce neat and crisp answers to the first two questions. Acknowledgedly it was insufficient to say that a book was *Bacon's Essays*. This would be a literary rather than a bibliographical description because the work has been so often reprinted since its first publication in 1597. An adequate bibliographical description would be produced when to the statement of author and title were added details of printer, place of printing, date and, in certain instances, a statement of edition. If, therefore, the work in question were to be specified as: '*Bacon*, Francis. "*The Essayes or Counsels*, Civill and Morall: With a Table of the Colours, or

Apparances (sic) of Good and Evill, and their Degrees, as places of Perswasion, and Disswasion, and their severall Fallaxes and the Elenches of them," the fifth complete edition, newly enlarged, printed in London by John Beale in 1639'; this would generally be regarded as setting this work sufficiently apart from all others to have an individual status. For many purposes, even in the more sophisticated bibliographical atmosphere of today, this kind of detail would still be sufficient. The difference now would be that it would be accepted as adequate against a background knowledge that a fuller analysis could extract more details if required. The amount of information contained above is virtually limited to that contained on the title-leaf. It is hardly surprising that many rudimentary bibliographers restricted themselves largely to title-leaf information. Traditionally the function of the title-leaf was to publicize just such information and, when supported by supplementary material gleaned from half-title leaves and prefatory matter, could be regarded as sufficient. Modern analysis has emphasized the critical importance of some of the newer areas of research and, particularly so, in those which contribute to the isolation of the copy.

At this point it is salutary to recall one of McKerrow's basic theses regarding the importance of understanding precisely what happens during the production of a book. 'The numerous processes through which all books pass are perfectly simple, and very little trouble will suffice for the understanding of them. What is needed is that they shall be grasped so clearly as to be constantly present to the mind of the student as he handles a book, so that he sees this not only from the point of view of the reader interested in it as literature, but also from the points of view of those who composed, corrected, printed, folded, and bound it; in short, so that he sees it not only as a unit, but as an assemblage of parts, each of which is the result of a clearly apprehended series of processes.'[1] McKerrow then proceeds to

[1] *McKERROW*, R. B. *An Introduction to Bibliography for Literary Students.* 1927. p. 4. (hereafter referred to as: *McKerrow: Introduction*)

outline these processes at the moment when 'a printer has a manuscript to print' and 'is about to begin the actual composition of the matter'. It is at this point when much modern work opens up a number of complexities in a hitherto simple concept. We are now very much concerned with the nature of the copy which the compositor had before him and the particular habits, vagaries, even the personality, of the compositor himself.

The relationship between these two aspects was clearly stated by Charlton Hinman in the introduction to his *The Printing and Proof-reading of the First Folio of Shakespeare*; '. . . the authority of any *printed* text will also depend upon how accurately the copy, whatsoever its nature, was reproduced in type. Even copy of small authority can be well printed; and copy of the very highest authority may be so carelessly reproduced, or reproduced by such unsatisfactory methods and by such incompetent workmen, that the text printed from it is seriously corrupt. Different kinds of copy, moreover, may be printed in different ways, so that some plays may be more likely than others to suffer textual change in the printing house. Hence the textual study of the First Folio, like Shakespearian textual study in general, is necessarily concerned with *two* main problems: the nature of the copy used by the printer; and the kinds and amount of modification to which this copy was subject during the printing process itself.'[1] Although Hinman's comments were limited to Shakespearian bibliographical work and many examples will necessarily come from this same field because nothing else has attracted a similar quantity of outstanding research, it is, nevertheless, equally true as a general statement throughout texts of all periods up to, and including, those of mid-twentieth century authors.

The magnitude of the problem, or perhaps more particularly the quality of work remaining to be done, can be judged if, against a list of major literary works, there were placed sure evidence as to the nature of the copy which the printer used.

[1] *HINMAN*, Charlton. *The Printing and Proof-reading of the First Folio of Shakespeare.* 2 vols. 1963. v. I. p. 5.

In the majority of cases a verdict of 'not proven' would be recorded and yet an appreciation of this kind is fundamental to the bibliographical analysis of the book. It is a problem of many ramifications.

In certain instances there may be a clear initial difficulty in attempting to ascertain the nature of such texts as might have been available even before the problem can be tackled of the nature of the actual copy itself which was used. This is of very obvious concern in the work of the early printers and the texts which were not contemporary with them. For example, when Caxton printed *The Canterbury Tales* in 1478, Chaucer had been dead for seventy-eight years and the work itself had probably been composed as long ago as about 1385. The date of an author's death is of obvious concern in such cases because it provides the clearest possible proof of the latest date at which any authorial changes could have been made. By the time that Caxton's first printing appeared there is ample evidence, in the shape of extant copies, that the work had multiplied in very many distinct but related manuscripts, and also that a considerable number of these were available in 1478. Whatever copy it was which the printer had in his office, it certainly could not have been one which was recently overseen and corrected by the author, and the balance of probability is against the availability of his own holograph, assuming that one ever existed. It is, nevertheless, possible on the evidence available to reach certain conclusions regarding the nature of the copy not only for the first printing but also for later printings. In 1924 Greg published his appreciation of the situation relating to the *Canterbury Tales* and, even if it now requires some adjustment or enlargement, it provides valuable evidence as to the kind of inferences which it is to be hoped could always be drawn.[1]

'To sum up, Caxton printed his first edition from a manuscript closely resembling, perhaps the immediate parent of, Tt[2]

---

[1] P.M.L.A. XXXIX, 4, December 1924. pp. 760–61.

[Camb. Trinity R. 3. 15], a somewhat peculiar manuscript belonging to a branch of the Corpus group. His second edition he printed from his first after it had been extensively altered by comparison with another manuscript whose affinities cannot be determined. Pynson printed his first edition from a copy of Caxton's second in which certain readings had been introduced from some manuscript of whose nature we know nothing. Pynson's second edition was printed from his first, but the copy used had been collated with Caxton's second (not however with the copy previously used) and a few readings introduced from a manuscript possibly of the Petworth group. Wynkyn de Worde printed his edition from Caxton's second and it is probable that he too had recourse to some manuscript source, though this cannot be identified. Lastly, Thynne's edition was printed by Godfray from that of de Worde, extensive alterations being again made by comparison with a manuscript. This manuscript may have been closely related to one now extant [$P\lambda^3$] which is classed as belonging to the Petworth group, though the readings disclose no particular affinities with manuscripts of this group in general, and it is quite likely that more than one manuscript was used.

'The following conclusions seem to be of interest. While Caxton's first edition was the only one set up from manuscript, the printers of the next five editions all had recourse more or less extensively to manuscript sources in the hope of improving their texts. It follows that Caxton's first edition alone ranks with the manuscripts as a textual authority. In no case can the readings of the manuscripts used in later editions be recovered with anything approaching completeness; the editions themselves are merely reprints of the first more or less seriously conflated, and their only textual value lies in the fact that they may possibly preserve individual readings from manuscripts but not found in any now extant. Lastly, the utter failure to identify the affinities of the manuscripts used in Caxton's second edition and in Thynne's, unless it be due to a plurality of sources, raises some doubt as to whether conflation may not be so wide spread as seriously to interfere with any useful classification of the manuscripts.'

If instances are taken of classical authors and their first appearance in print then the situation is obviously exaggerated. E. P. Goldschmidt explored this problem in his *Medieval Texts and their First Appearance in Print*, and the tenuous link which existed between the first printed text and an authoritive manuscript was demonstrated in many examples.[1] Among the early printers there were assuredly those who exhibited great concern to ensure that the copy of an older work which they used was as authentic as possible. To them we owe a considerable debt of gratitude not simply for the fact that some works have been preserved at all, but also that many of them were made available in editions which were most scrupulously and judiciously edited. Caxton was obviously delighted to be presented with what was alleged to be a more authoritative manuscript when he printed his second edition of the *Canterbury Tales*. The early sixteenth-century scholar printers at their best demonstrated a commendable enthusiasm in the pursuit of good manuscripts. The arrival of Greek scholars in Italy at the close of the fifteenth and the early part of the sixteenth centuries played a large part in the textual work of the Renaissance printers and deeply influenced the availability of scholars to do the necessary work for their presses.

Consequently, the tradition was well established among some categories of printers that it was a matter of concern to them which copy was used by the press, certainly in so far as classical or non-contemporary authors were involved.

As the sixteenth century progressed the emphasis became more and more firmly fixed on the production of contemporary works. The author was available in the sense that he was alive. Whether he would be likely to take a direct interest in the printing of his works was another question. The likelihood was, on the whole, probably a matter of individual choice, although

---

[1] GOLDSCHMIDT, E. P. *Medieval Texts and their First Appearance in Print.* 1943.

certain categories, the Court poets for example, were almost certainly not involved in anything which might suggest a pecuniary interest from their Muse. Similarly, H. S. Bennett wrote, many years ago, that no evidence existed that any Elizabethan dramatist took the slightest interest in the printing of his works. It would be extremely difficult to generalize although some suggestions can certainly be made along these lines. If, however, the author, although living, took no direct interest in publication, from what various sources could the manuscript have come to keep presses alive during these years of great activity? Probably no single question looms more largely over late sixteenth- and early seventeenth-century bibliography.

There have been signs from time to time that editors in general have ranged from a total disregard of the status of the copy through an unswerving belief in the accuracy of any copy, to a deep rooted suspicion that all printers were rogues and all manuscripts corrupt. Any attempt at generalization, either for a person or for a particular type of work, would founder on the evidence. Each period of printing, from the beginnings up to and through the present age, can produce examples of care in the choice of copy just as it can of lax habits. In the long run the integrity of the printer and the editor will affect the issue as much as any other single factor and each case must, therefore, be approached entirely afresh. It is by no means easy to produce any quantity of cases in which the *exact* nature of the copy can be *proved* with any certainty.

A slightly different situation occurs when it can be demonstrated, with varying degrees of certainty, that one printing of a book has been set up from a previous edition. Although the question of the copy for the original printing may still be left in doubt, the copy for the particular issue can sometimes be determined. In such instances, interest will centre upon the possibility or likelihood of authorial corrections having been made which may account for variations in the text between the printings. For this reason particular importance is attached to the editions published during an author's lifetime and due regard paid to the probability of his having a direct hand in any amendments. Cases of this nature are probably very frequent since as McKerrow said, 'It may then generally be *assumed* that a later edition is printed from an earlier one unless there is clear evidence to the contrary; but one can often get direct evidence of the fact.'[1]

A third form of copy becomes a possiblity following the rise of periodical and serial publication and in the nineteenth century was relatively frequent. In cases when a work originally appeared in periodical form it was common practice for the book text to be set up from the periodical text, sometimes from the galley proofs. In this latter case the proofs might or might not be revised and, consequently, the authority and the nature of any corrections needs to be taken into account.

The chief probable sources of copy are therefore, three in number: (a) manuscripts, of variable authority, but usually only for first printings; (b) a previously published edition, with or without corrections; and (c) particularly in the nineteenth and twentieth centuries, printings for serial or periodical publications, sometimes in the form of galley proofs and, sometimes, unrevised. These are, naturally, all broad categories and within each there is a wide range of authority and integrity. It is a problem which is always central to any critical approach to a book and one on which the bibliographer is forced to try and come to some conclusion.

The business of analytical bibliography is to throw as much light as possible on all the stages in the transmission of the text, which, in effect, means upon each step in the production of the printed versions. Next in chronological order in the sequence, as it were, following the problems of the copy, is the analysis of the work of the compositor. The methods of the compositor have become fairly well known in modern times as a part of the generally increased knowledge of printing house practice. In recent years much of the advance has been in the measures

---

[1] *McKERROW: Introduction.* p. 187.

which have led to the identification of the characteristics of individual compositors as evidenced in the books themselves.

One of the first noteworthy attempts to establish the pattern of compositor practice in the printing house was that of Professor J. Dover Wilson in 1934 with the publication of his *The Manuscript of Shakespeare's Hamlet*. This opened up the period of the next thirty years during which Dr Alice Walker's *Textual Problems of the First Folio* in 1953 was a major contribution and the culminating point, to date, has been Charlton Hinman's monumental *Printing and Proofreading of the First Folio* in 1963. *The Transactions of the Bibliographical Society* and, notably during the last twenty years, *Studies in Bibliography* have throughout this time published the results of a considerable number of investigations in this area. As a result of these the kind of compositorial pattern which could have obtained in printing books of this period has become much more definite. A high percentage of the studies have been within the field of Shakespearian studies but this does not invalidate the findings in a larger context.

Analysis has now made it quite clear that there would frequently, perhaps usually, be more than one compositor working on the text of a book. Compositorial activities are central to every attempt at understanding the nature of the printed text. As Dr Walker wrote, 'Even if a text was printed from autograph which reached the printer as Shakespeare left it, we have always to reckon with the fallibility of the compositor in reproducing his copy.'[1] Each compositor would be different from his colleagues in a number of respects. One might be extremely meticulous in all that he did while another might be slap-dash by nature and a third might be young and comparatively inexperienced. The first problem is to try and distinguish between the work of the various compositors and to build up as full a picture as possible of the particular strength and weaknesses of each. If this pattern can be built up in depth then

---

[1] *WALKER*, Alice. *Textual Problems of the First Folio.* 1953. p. 122.

future problems can be determined against the known characteristics of a particular compositor. Only in this way will it ever be possible to judge which errors might be attributed to the copy and which to the compositor. Although this is an oversimplification of the issues involved, and compositorial analysis is never an easy step in the elucidation of bibliographical problems, it does, nevertheless, state the desirable objectives. Such an analysis is, on many occasions, an essential preliminary to a more detailed investigation.

Spelling provides one of the most substantial forms of evidence in the identification of individual compositors in spite of the fact that the whole question of spelling in books of this period has been insufficiently investigated. An appearance of well-nigh anarchy in spelling habits is occasionally presented by some texts. Yet it is at least possible that we are witnessing, throughout the late years of the sixteenth and early seventeenth centuries, an attempt to formulate conventions in printing house spelling. Progressively, therefore, we can trace the slow establishment of order. Spelling will, nevertheless, provide the most certain clues, even if they do not constitute proof.

On the basis of evidence such as this Alice Walker postulated the existence in the printing house for the First Folio of two compositors with widely differing characteristics: 'Compositor A was, in general, the more attentive and the more faithful to copy. B was less conservative and more slap-dash, carried more in his head than he could memorize, omitted lines and words more frequently, and was more prone to memorial substitution and even deliberate bodging.'[1] When the reconstruction of a compositor's attitudes can be so detailed there is obviously a basis for the evaluation of inconsistencies and errors in disputed passages.

Charlton Hinman's study has notably added to the detail which we possess regarding printing house practice in general and compositorial work in particular. Hinman collated, with the

---

[1] *ibid.* p. 11.

aid of his collating machine, more than fifty copies of the First Folio. Using the evidence of type, spelling, headlines and all the whole range of bibliographical points he was able to distinguish the work of five compositors. Four of these remain rather indefinite in their outline but compositor E begins to assume a clear identity. Hinman was able to demonstrate conclusively that this fifth compositor was an apprentice, permitted to set only from printed copy and not from manuscript. Since Jaggard had only one apprentice, John Leason, we are at last in the position of being able to name one compositor of the First Folio. Hinman's work also cast considerable light on the methods of the proof-reading of the text. The conclusion reached here is that much of the correction which was made was for purposes of correcting literal errors which, in the majority of instances, would not necessitate any consultation of the copy.

Hinman's biggest surprise, however, was his discovery that the work was not set page by page as might be at first assumed. The book is a folio in sixes; that is, after correct imposition and printing, a gathering is made up by putting three folded sheets one inside another. The outside sheet thus has pages 1 and 12 on its outer side and 2 and 11 on the inner. The inmost sheet has pages 5 and 8 on its outer side and 6 and 7 on the inner. Each pair of pages was printed from a forme of type. Two compositors, working together on a gathering, would proceed as follows: one would set page 6 and one page 7. The former would then follow 6 with 5, 4, 3, 2, 1, while the latter would continue with 8, 9, 10, 11 and 12. This would entail careful casting off but, even so, the compositor who was working backwards would meet problems in completely filling in the space available with any accuracy.

Researches into the problems of identification of copy and the analysis of compositorial work have gone a long way towards establishing the scope of analytical bibliographical work and in demonstrating how detailed an investigation can be carried out when the circumstances dictate. Beyond this point the bibliographer is faced very directly with the tangible evidence of the book itself. Many of the further problems which arise in analysis are far from being simple of solution and they call for a thorough understanding of exactly what it is reasonable to regard as bibliographical evidence. A debate has raged during the past quarter of a century on the exact nature of bibliographical evidence and the conclusions which may legitimately be drawn from it. Agreement may never be reached on this issue since the point at which bibliographical evidence begins to merge and to coalesce with historical, linguistic and literary evidence is a very indeterminate one. Two clear steps, however, are necessary as a basis to all other study and of these there can be no doubt at all as to their essentially bibliographical nature.

No worthwhile or lasting conclusions can be made regarding any publication until it can be demonstrated, beyond any reasonable shadow of doubt, that it is what it purports to be. This is no place to raise a false or misleading scent about forgeries and such like. It would be wrong to suggest that even the majority of instances when false dates are being investigated could possibly be glamorized by the term forgeries. Unhappily too much attention has been devoted to this narrow field of work and a sense of proportion has been lost. Nevertheless, if a printing can clearly be shown to be of a given date and if, additionally, it is whole and perfect, then firm ground can be said to exist for a more detailed study. Although the solution of any problems of dating may not reach far beyond that particular piece of information it will, at least, identify the specific work which is under review. A critical area of analysis of the book must, therefore, be associated with its correct dating and its completeness.

There are many ways of verifying the apparent date of printing of a book or of ascribing a date to an undated book. However tentative the final suggested date may be, it is certainly an analysis which will illuminate many aspects of the book. Initially, it would be foolish in the extreme not to check the entry in standard bibliographical works. Although this is a process of devolving on to other shoulders the problem which is truly one's own, it is a sensible preliminary provided that it is approached with caution. The amount of meticulous scholarship which has gone to create, for example, the British Museum's *Catalogue of Books Printed in the XVth Century* cannot be matched in many libraries any more readily than a similar collection can be discovered elsewhere. In a different field the same circumstances attended the publication of Harvard University's *Catalogue of French Sixteenth Century Books*. Both for the nature of the collections as well as for the editorial scholarship, bibliographical catalogues such as these cannot easily be matched. The great libraries of the world have produced printed catalogues which are repositories of an immense quantity and variety of accurate detail. The same quality of important material may be found in the sale catalogues of some of the leading booksellers and book auction rooms. In each case the catalogue is a cumulation of collections and experience garnered over very many years and it is obviously sound policy that such tools should be used to the utmost. While checking against such catalogues it is natural that precautions must be taken against catalogues and bibliographies which are known to be incomplete or inaccurate. Warnings are so often sounded against Wise's *Ashley Library Catalogue* on account of the forgeries now known to be included. Because of these it needs handling with excessive care but equally it would be foolish to ignore completely the amount of good bibliographical work which it also contains. Other bibliographies will be used with caution because of the amount of work which has been done within the field since publication, but only a small handful can be totally ignored.

Apart from this preliminary, the main assault must be on the book itself. Some peripheral information may be of concern. such as the dating of author, editor, translator, illustrator and so on, but on the whole such details are liable to be much more broadly based than the problem. In many cases the actual date of printing is only an auxiliary factor to the sequence of printings of a particular work. Consequently, datings are frequently required within somewhat narrow limitations whereas these which are suggested give broad indications.

Identification of printer and, subsequently, the hope of being able to place books correctly within the sequence of his own printing, is always crucial but fraught with problems. Biographical information which is readily accessible about printers is limited in the extreme. They figure but rarely and briefly in the main national biographical dictionaries and there are few special dictionaries which are devoted to the members of the book trade. Examples of the latter category which do exist, such as the Bibliographical Society's series covering members of the British book trade up to 1775, are only partial listings and in need of revision. In spite of such poverty of biographical information a student frequently finds that he is advised to check against the dates of activity of a printer or the period during which one worked at a particular address. Such purely historical reconstruction is the life blood of analytical bibliography which sets out to establish the whole background and biography of a book. One most fruitful source of such information would be the full indexing of the imprints in some major bibliographical publications. The extent to which this provides an entry to this type of detail can be judged by studying Paul G. Morrison's Indexes to the S.T.C. and Wing.[1] These should be compared and contrasted with the variety and amount of information which is produced and made available when the problem of the imprint is approached on its own. An example, and an extremely good one, of this approach to the problem is Marcus A. McCorison's *Vermont imprints 1778–1820*.[2] Regional and highly localized studies of this nature are likely to be among the most productive in furthering the ends of this kind of

[1] *MORRISON*, Paul G. *Index of Printers, Publishers and Booksellers in . . . S.T.C. . . .* 1950.
Index of Printers, Publishers and Booksellers in Donald Wing's S.T.C. . . . 1955.
[2] *McCORISON*, Marcus A. *Vermont imprints, 1778–1820; a check list of books, pamphlets, and broadsides.* 1963.

research. It is primarily within such limited contexts that a search in depth could be conducted to produce the relevant background of information. Although the Vermont volume is not an isolated example, such studies are all too few and many more are needed before we can begin to say with any certainty that we can utilize biographical material on printers, publishers and booksellers in our search.

Possible identification of the printer and some indication of the particular phase of his work in which a book appeared may be forthcoming as a result of an analysis of his technical materials and procedures. It was in such an approach that modern bibliography really had its origins. The science and study of palaeography had for generations been pursued with an increasingly high level of accuracy. By the time that the new bibliography began to establish itself in the nineteenth century palaeographic studies could 'date' handwriting without undue risk of error. Many of the early bibliographers were palaeographers both by training and by instinct and it was naturally towards typography that they turned their analytical eyes. Such typographic studies had a natural relationship with palaeography since the early type designs were in a natural line of descent from the book hands of the period. On this basis Bradshaw, Proctor, Haebler and those who, with just cause, have been named as the earliest proto-typographers came to many of their judgements. The strength and usefulness of the method came because this was the most rapidly changing aspect of the book in the early days of printing and the one which was, at that stage, liable to be the most individual to the printer. In later periods typography became of less importance as type designs were more standardized, although at periods of important changes and developments or in the instances of markedly individual printers it can still provide a most fruitful line of approach. As the value of this kind of evidence diminishes other aspects become increasingly important. For example, the use of woodcut borders on title-pages and at chapter headings and endings was sufficiently widespread in the sixteenth

century and yet the use of an individual cut sufficiently restricted in its use to provide valuable evidence. The same kind
of role is played by printers' factota, flowers and ornaments in
the eighteenth century. Until the advent of the vast typographical and flower designs from the great corporations, such
as Monotype and Linotype, at the end of the nineteenth century, there was still considerable individuality in the use of
typographical material by a single printer. This vitally assists
the process of identification and also the possibility of assigning
priorities to successive printings.

When all other species of evidence have been considered
there is one area which increasingly appears to be fruitful in the
light of current investigation. Assuming the field of printed
books, it can be safely asserted that all but a tiny handful were
printed on paper. All evidence to date suggests that the normal
practice, as common sense would indicate, would be for a
printer to use paper fairly soon after delivery. In turn, this
would probably be soon after manufacture because there was
nothing to be gained by delay either at the paper mill or at the
printer's. At all periods, paper has been a proportionately
expensive item in the whole process of the making of the book.
Special consideration must be given to those situations in which
paper had to travel long distances between mill and printer.
This contingency arises when local manufacture has not yet
begun and paper has to be imported. A case in point would be
the whole of printing in North America from its inception in
1640 until paper-making began there in 1690. Even when such
a date can be established for native paper-making it did not
usually herald a flood of material and a rapid closure to im-
ports. Consequently for a considerable period in most printing
centres a wide variety of papers can be discovered. This is a
circumstance which adds a range of possible evidence for the
bibliographer to study in relation to a book or to the work of a
press. It also indicates some of the circumstances of paper usage
which can make it possible to date the paper and then, within
reasonably close limits, to ascribe a date to the book.

There are two main approaches to the problem of the dating of paper. There have been developments in the manufacturing processes of paper throughout its history and changes in the ingredients from which it is made. There is, consequently, always the possibility of arriving at a date through a chemical analysis of the paper. The disadvantages lie in the relative infrequency with which any such material changes have taken place and also the comparatively broad periods of time into which it could arrange the products. From the beginnings of paper making onward for many centuries there were no significant changes. Indeed until our knowledge of the rags which were used for many centuries is more detailed than at present, it is difficult to isolate many developments in use of materials which might have produced significant differences in the papers until the late eighteenth century. With the discovery of chlorine and the manufacture of bleaching agents a first considerable step was taken. On the other hand it is only in cases of careless manufacture that any probability of detection exists in the finished product. The early nineteenth-century papers began to add fresh possibilities as new types of loading agents were added to papers in order to secure added whiteness and smoothness. The early part of the second half added yet more evidence as the newer materials of wood pulps, esparto grass and straw began to replace the less economically practical rags. Obviously, so few critical changes in manufacture cannot provide a great number of points of reference in connection with dating. Nevertheless this kind of evidence was crucial in the uncovering of the Wise pamphlets and it would, therefore, be unrealistic to avoid mention of it entirely.

A more accurate and conclusive kind of assistance is provided by the ability to date paper through an examination which stops short of chemical analysis. Ever since 1282 the majority of book papers have been watermarked. The piece of wire twisted and soldered on to the base of the paper-maker's frame had a life of limited duration. When it needed renewal there was no reason at all why a paper-maker should seek to make a new mark in the exact lineaments of the old. Even within that period of duration which, according to Briquet is unlikely to be more than fifteen years at the outside, the water-mark would show signs of progressive deterioration and decay.[1] Within the lifetime of what one paper-maker might, therefore, consider as *one* design, there could be several states of a water-mark as it was renewed and also indications of sequence within each state. An analysis of one individual watermark listed in any of the major bibliographical surveys will indicate how this pattern might emerge. Apart from the records of the paper mills which, when they exist, might produce some evidence as to the period of use of a particular mark, there is above every-thing else the evidence of the books themselves. From the moment when watermarking began and especially so by the time that the printed book began to appear nearly two hundred years later, the majority of books were dated. There is no reason to suspect that anything more than a tiny fraction were in-correctly dated. Consequently, it has been possible to establish lists of watermarks indicating the dates of their known usage. This will enable some approach to be made to the problem of an undated book which has a watermarked paper. It can only be an approach, because it would be misleading to suggest that all the world's watermarks have been recorded in this manner. Currently this is far from so. One of the difficulties, apart from that of shortage of labourers within the field, has been that of making the actual record of the mark. The leaf had to be held up to a strong source of light and a drawing made of the mark. This was slow, laborious and with great possibilities of error. As recently as 1960, however, the Academy of Sciences of the USSR published details of a revolutionary new method of recording watermarks.[2] This is the use of β-radiographic prints

[1] *BRIQUET*, C. M. *Les Filigranes.* . . . 2nd ed. 4. vols 1923.

[2] The first English account of this method, referring to the original Russian text, may be found in:

SIMMONS, J. S. G. *The Leningrad method of watermark reproduction.* In 'The Book Collector', Autumn 1961, pp. 329–30. *illus.*

of the marks which entirely disregard the print on the pages. The system has since been used in England and notably by Allan Stevenson, with the results exhibited in the British Museum in 1967. This development has opened up considerable new possibilities in this field. Allan Stevenson's name has become inextricably associated with the use of paper evidence in bibliographical work in the post-war years and his writings and his investigations, notably on the *Constance Missal* and the Vinland Map, provide valuable proof of the efficacy of the methods.[1]

In addition to the feasibility of being able to date an individual piece of paper there is another fact about the usual make-up of a book. In many instances a book is printed on mixed stocks of paper. There may be, in a book of any size, as many as ten different makes of paper with as many watermarks. Assuming that each watermark and each state of each mark is capable of being assigned to a particular period, then by process of overlapping dates the date of the book itself can be narrowed to yet more precise limits.

In addition to any evidence such as the foregoing which might eventuate in a specific date for a piece of printing, there is also the possiblity of being able to put a series of printings in their chronological sequence. From this result it may also prove possible to suggest which printed texts were used as the copies for any later printing. This assumes the validity of the idea that, apart from the first printing, subsequent printings will normally be set up from a printed text rather than afresh from a manuscript. The book itself may bear indications of this relationship between printings. It is not uncommon to find editions which state specifically that they are 'first edition' or 'second edition'. Others may take the situation a little further and list the sequence of impressions, with occasionally in post-1800 books, the number of copies within each edition. Such information cannot be relied upon specifically, for publishers'

[1] *STEVENSON*, Allan. *The Problem of the Missale Speciale.* 1967.
SKELTON, R. A., *MARSTON*, Thomas E., and *PAINTER*, George D. *The Vinland Map and the Tartar Relation.* 1965.

accuracy in such matters varies widely. There is also a problem
in the case of non-copyright material, especially when several
publishers are issuing the works of an author and recording
their own sequence of printings only. The successful end of the
trail, however, in ascribing dates and in putting a series of books
into their correct order still does not complete the assignment.
The object of this kind of arrangement is primarily that of
indicating the basic bibliographical relationships of the texts
between one printing and another, and the ordering of the
edition will not do this by itself. Only a small number of editors,
of any kind of text, have been persuaded, or are naturally inclined, to put the details of their establishment of a text among
their prefatory material. Much of the evidence relating to this
particular aspect of the problem must be associated with the
text itself.

So far, the examination of the book will, it is hoped, have
yielded certain specific pieces of information about the work
in hand. Initially, it may prove extremely difficult to give
much more than absolutely basic information about the book,
but it should prove possible to describe the copy as being something more than just such and such a work or even such an
edition or printing of a work. Proceeding beyond these basic
details it should distinguish it as a copy with such a sequence
of variants and with such cancels. It must, in fact, be a general
process of establishing more and more clearly the individuality
of the copy. In the long run this is the main purpose of the
process of collation. Step by step it sets off this one copy from
all others of the same work. In the end, this will culminate in
matters relating to the particular condition of the copy.

Initially, the most important single feature about a copy of a
book is whether or not it is complete. Deductions of any kind
made from an incomplete copy, in common with deductions
made from any limited amount of material, have only limited
validity. Modern investigations of books such as Charlton
Hinman's have made it ever more difficult to come easily to
conclusions because it cannot be assumed that a missing portion

will be identical with the similar portion from another copy. First, however, the completeness or otherwise of a particular copy must be demonstrated.

From a bibliographical viewpoint completeness as a term means something quite specific. It is the copy exactly as it was intended to be by the printer or publisher at the moment of publication. In other words, it is neither imperfect in the sense that its condition has deteriorated from that moment, nor have defects been 'made good' so that the copy becomes 'made perfect'. If there are imperfections in the copy, which by comparison with other copies seem to have been there at the moment of publication, then these defects can be explained as 'state' rather than as 'condition'. The bibliographer can start from the premise that only full sheets of a known and given size would have been placed on the machine in the first place. In this examination of the book, therefore, he should be able to 'imagine' the whole of the sheet as laid out in front of him. For him to be able to adjudge a book as complete he should be able to account, normally by its presence in the copy, for every part of the sheet which went to the press.

It does not necessarily follow that each sheet will remain perfectly intact within the book. Certain formats and the usual way in which the book was made up would preclude this. Because of this, the bibliographer must be completely familiar with the commonest formats of particular periods and the normal methods of make-up. A folio will only very rarely be sewn throughout the book in pairs of conjugate leaves each constituting a gathering. Although the make-up of a folio in fours, or sixes, or eights does not involve any change in the individual sheet, it is a convention in book building which affects the whole study of a book. Similarly, the normal gatherings of quartos and octavos leave the basic sheet whole, but with duodecimos a new situation is reached. Although many duodecimos can be found which were sewn in gatherings of twelve leaves, that is, with the sheet intact, many books of this format have had the original sheet cut and sewn up in sixes or in alternate eights and fours. Whether the sheet is intact or whether it has been cut, but withal is still present in all its parts, the problem remains for the bibliographer to demonstrate that everything is there as intended. Normally, the book, as intended to be issued by the publisher, will have all the sheets as complete as when they went on to the press. Only in the case of cancels may one part actually be missing, although this is not always necessarily so of every kind of cancel.

If following the first part of the examination there remains little or no doubt as to the exact identification of the work and, following the second part, an assurance that the work in question is complete, then deductions can be made. They may be deductions which are concerned specifically with the bibliographical nature of the book and, therefore, to be recorded in the description or with facts relating to the textual material itself and consequently liable to have a bearing on the study of the text.

4
Descriptive bibliography

The description of an item is a logical step to follow upon the complete analysis of a book and the solution of its bibliographical problems. The results of the analysis are set down in some predetermined order in order to reveal the bibliographical nature of the book. No description of any value can possibly be produced until the critical analysis of the book has been completed. The descriptive bibliography is a development, or further stage in the evolution, of the hand-list or catalogue and will, therefore, share some of the problems which have been discussed in connection with systematic bibliography. A descriptive bibliography differs from an enumerative or systematic bibliography in respect of the quantity and kind of detail which is included. It will usually treat of the bibliographical aspects of a book in a detail which is unnecessary, and undesirable, at enumerative level and, consequently, the resultant tool is of use for quite different purposes. It should never be suggested, or assumed, that descriptive work is, in some strange fashion, 'better' or 'more advanced' than systematic work in any sense which could be construed as pejorative to the latter. It is different and complementary but no more.

The elements of a description can be seen in any student's manual of bibliography and are usually regarded as consisting of seven parts: the heading; the full transcript of the title-page; the collation entry; the art collation; the page by page description; facts regarding the work as a whole *and* facts relating to this particular copy.[1] This is a good point from which to make a beginning. A record of a description must have some kind of basic pattern to it, if it is to be intelligible to as wide a body of users as possible. On the other hand, it would be dangerous and misleading to suggest that every bibliographical description of every book for every known purpose should contain exactly these elements in that pre-determined order. The purpose of a description is to convey as precise a record of the book as the occasion demands. It must, therefore, be expected that occasions will arise when the order of the parts themselves will need some kind of adjustment; it should certainly never be regarded as sacrosanct. Naturally there will be instances when the material for one part of the description is absent in the book itself; for example, an absence of anything which might be regarded as claiming the attention of an art collation or any noteworthy features regarding the work as a whole. It would be absurd to force facts into a description merely because space can be found for them. If they are irrelevant to the true function of the description, then they should be excluded. These are clear-cut cases. In others it is matter of opinion. In a plate-book, for example, it can frequently be assumed that the art collation will be the main reason for taking any bibliographical interest in the book at all. Consequently, it is only to be expected that the art collation will be given some prominence and when necessary brought out of its order as one of the seven parts. In the case of a description of an item in a bookseller's catalogue then the first six parts are frequently a general background to the final part, the facts relating to this particular copy. The bookseller's cataloguer is producing the right kind of description for the book in question if he brings out these facts as major elements in his description. It is, after all, this particular copy and none other which he is offering for sale. The bibliographer has the responsibility to decide upon the relative importance of the items within the description and to arrange them so as to reveal

[1] This is discussed in more detail in:
STOKES, Roy. *Esdaile's Manual of Bibliography.* 1967. *Chapter* 10.

the greatest amount possible about the book. Equally he has clear control as to the extent of material which he puts into his description. It is not good policy to overload a description with unnecessary detail but, equally, much effort is wasted if there is inadequate information. The amount and detail of the information is less likely to be determined by the bibliographical, historical, literary or monetary status of the book itself than by the function of the list. Caxton's first printing of *The Canterbury Tales* is a work which occupies an important place in all four respects, but this does not mean that a description will be equally detailed whenever and wherever it exists. In the S.T.C. it occupies a modest four lines which is less than the space occupied by many works which have only tenuous claims on all four counts. The purpose of the listing, however, in the S.T.C. is quite clear; it is purely for the fundamental purpose of listing and locating English books up to 1640. It is to be expected that a completely different description would appear of the same work in Gordon Duff's *Fifteenth Century English Books* and in Seymour de Ricci's *Census of Caxtons*.[1] In these two later instances not only is the scope of the bibliography very much more restricted, but the purpose becomes increasingly bibliographical in intention.

Similarly the entry for the Shakespeare First Folio in the *Cambridge Bibliography of English Literature* is entirely adequate. It records the fact that the first collected edition of Shakespeare's plays was issued in 1623. No details are given beyond this because none is necessary. The bibliography has an entirely literary purpose in view and the record of the date is sufficient. The S.T.C., with its strong bibliographical purpose produces the additional basic bibliographical information in twelve lines. When the stage of Greg's *A Bibliography of the English Printed Drama to the Restoration* is reached then the description covers four pages. At even that comparatively extended treatment it proved impossible for Greg to include all the important biblio-

[1] *DUFF*, E. Gordon. *Fifteenth Century English Books*. 1917.
DE RICCI, Seymour. *A Census of Caxtons*. 1909.

graphical detail. The remainder spilled over into the 468 pages of his separate work on the First Folio.[1] Even now, after the absorption of another thousand-odd pages of argument regarding the bibliography of this work from Charlton Hinman, the last word most certainly has not been written. The description in the *Cambridge Bibliography* is, in spite of all this, still a perfectly accurate and adequate description for its purpose. It successfully sets this one printing of Shakespeare's collected works apart from the others. Nothing more should be asked of it.

In each of these instances, *The Canterbury Tales* or the First Folio, the book remains the same; the purpose of the bibliography varies.

Similar variation may be found in another important respect. There is obviously a very close connection between a bibliography and the printed catalogue of a library where the collection is of sufficient importance for its catalogue to become regarded as an important bibliographical tool. A case in point is the published *Catalogue of Books Printed in the XVth Century now in the British Museum*.[2] In default of the presence of any completed bibliography of incunabula, this British Museum catalogue ranks as the major printed catalogue within this field from any important library. Accordingly, it has over the years been accepted as the major bibliographical tool and used accordingly. Nevertheless its true status is that of a catalogue. The entries describe specific copies of the books in question and, whatever reference may be made to copies in other libraries, this basic fact is not changed.

A bibliography of incunabula, in the very strict sense of the word, would necessarily have a different approach. No *one* copy would be under review but rather that to which Fredson Bowers has accorded the title of the 'ideal copy'. Each successive piece of modern bibliographical research has made it abundantly

[1] GREG, W. W. *The Shakespeare First Folio its bibliographical and textual history.* 1955.

[2] *BRITISH MUSEUM, Catalogue of Books Printed in the XVth Century now in the British Museum.* 1908 – *in progress.*

more clear that no two copies of early printed books can be assumed to be identical. The sense of uniqueness of the individual copy within a printing is nowhere more marked than among incunabula. The whole process of printing was at such an experimental stage and so individual to each participant that minute, but frequently important, differences proliferated. These differences arose, however, within a common frame of intention on the part of the printer or publisher. There can be little doubt but that, if he had been able to do so, he would have produced identical copies on the morning of publication. Although he failed, sometimes miserably, in that intention yet we can assume that there was an ideal state towards which he was hopefully heading. Many of the variations which exist between extant copies are, in fact, the results of his successive attempts to reach that particular state. In a bibliography, therefore, as opposed to a catalogue, it is clearly the responsibility of the bibliographer to describe the book in that state in which the printer or publisher had hoped and intended that it would appear. In short, he should prepare to describe the 'ideal copy'. The situation may well be complicated for him by the fact that the ideal copy is not, in fact, represented by any extant copy and he will, consequently, be describing a work as it is not known currently to exist.

This difference in approach arises because of the distinction in function between a bibliography and a catalogue in that the latter is concerned with the actual copies in a particular collection. Nevertheless there are many occasions when the details of the copy available for cataloguing in a collection are not sufficient for any significant bibliographical usage of the copy. The clearest instance of this would be with the case of an imperfect copy, and the situation becomes even clearer if it is assumed that a title-leaf is missing. Both description and book have very limited usage if nothing is done to remedy the loss. Provided the copy for description is not unique the title-leaf should be available, even if not inserted, in facsimile and a description produced in accordance with available evidence. A catalogue which did no more than record a missing part, with no attempt to provide the missing text in facsimile in the collection, would be inadequate in practice. The library must, from time to time, admit the inadequacy of the material which it houses. The catalogue, and especially a bibliographical catalogue must reflect this concern. A good case can be substantiated for a library catalogue, when concerned with rare or important material, to describe the 'ideal copy' and note the library's own variations from that, rather than to catalogue the item itself.

It soon becomes apparent that, in descriptive bibliography, the bibliographer is working primarily from experience rather than with the assistance of carefully compiled rules. It can indeed be argued that the only rule in descriptive bibliography is that there are no rules. In the light of his own and others' accumulated knowledge of a particular field a bibliographer must work out his own salvation with due regard to the purpose of the list. There are many guides but no rule-books. In the long run, in conjunction with personal experience however halting and imperfect initially, nothing instructs so well as excellence. It is for this reason that the methods adopted in some of the major descriptive bibliographies should be looked to in order to provide instructive examples.

Not surprisingly, the fullest and most modest appraisal of the problems facing the bibliographer when he comes face to face with his individual responsibility can be found in the introduction to the best example of modern descriptive work. At the end of sixty years of work, Greg wrote the 'Introduction' to his Restoration drama bibliography. In it he described how his own methods had developed during this time.

'My aim in this introduction is to explain the lines on which the present work has been prepared and so to enable a reader, by a full understanding of the details, to make the best use of it. The need for precise and uniform presentation of bibliographical facts has necessitated the adoption of many conventions, the exact significance of which may not always be immediately apparent. In the following pages I have tried to furnish all the information that can be required by a reader already acquainted with the elements of the subject. I have not of course tried to write a comprehensive treatise on bibliographical description, but if any reader is in difficulty over matters here assumed to be familiar, he will always I think find the necessary information in McKerrow's *Introduction to Bibliography for Literary Students*. At the same time the account I have to give of the manner in which the various problems of description have been tackled should throw some incidental light on the practices respecting printing and publication current in the sixteenth and seventeenth centuries and even to some extent on the wider problems of the censoring and licensing of plays.

'Before embarking on further explanations I had better make a personal explanation. The methods adopted in this bibliography are the outcome of some sixty years' experience and consideration. But during that period they have grown by a natural process of elaboration as fresh problems were encountered and fresh expedients devised to meet them, and these expedients have inevitably been conditioned by the immediate circumstances and adopted with less regard than would have been ideally desirable to theoretical considerations and meticulous consistency. It has been only too often a case of *solvitur ambulando*. If, with my present experience and with the technical tradition now available to the bibliographer, I were now starting my task afresh – which heaven forbid! – I should doubtless adopt a system of description in some respects different from that followed in these volumes. But habits get ingrained, and when work has proceeded throughout a life-time it would perhaps be too much to demand that it should be recast in the interests of a theoretically more perfect system, even if it had not already reached the damning finality of print. I can only trust that what defects of method persist – for much has of course been revised – will not be found to detract to any serious degree from the usefulness of the work, and only ask that whatever inconsistencies of execution are found may be pardoned. I have now and then, in the course of my explanations, added a note warning readers that I should not now advocate a particular usage adopted. But with such exceptions I hope that the methods that I have found serviceable in my own work may prove of wider use, and that in them may be found, if not a standard to follow, at least a pattern from which other bibliographers may find it convenient to borrow whatever should prove of assistance in their own fields. At the same time, lest anyone should think that looking back on my work I feel any complacency over the manner of its execution, I here admit that I can hear the caustic critic who ever sits like a familiar imp at my elbow maintaining that my problem in writing this introduction has been threefold: first to discover what in fact I have done, next why I did it, and lastly how best it may be defended.'

These are certainly not the words of a man who considered that he had reached finality in his methods. Even after sixty years, during which time there had been no particular model for him to follow, he could not feel that he had evolved a system for others. There was nothing more than 'a pattern from which other bibliographers may find it convenient to borrow'. But for all the modest disclaimer it can never be doubted but that McKerrow's elaboration of the principles of bibliographical investigation, followed by Greg's extraordinary success in codifying the principles of description in practice more than in theory, placed descriptive bibliography on a firm basis. Since their time both theory and practice have been taken further.

The foundations of modern bibliographical description, and especially so within the field of incunabula, were firmly established in 1826 when Ludwig Hain published the first volume of his *Repertorium Bibliographicum*.[1] It is arguable that they set a standard from which no radical departure has since been made and, therefore, that standardization of entry has been a fact for well over a century. In the broadest possible terms this is undoubtedly true yet, as has already become apparent in the

[1] *HAIN*, Ludwig F. T. *Repertorium Bibliographicum ad Annum MD*. 2 vols. in 4. 1826–1838.

work of Greg, much refinement has already been accomplished and much more remains to be done. We live in an age of standardization and the rogue elephant is widely accepted as being a menace to the well-being of the whole herd. It is possible that we have travelled a little too far, or perhaps too rapidly, along the road which might lead to standardization of bibliographical description. When Curt Bühler wrote his chapter on 'Incunabula' in the volume on *Standards of Bibliographical Description* in 1949, he said then that, 'A difficulty which should be recognized at the outset is that incunabulists have, in general, pursued their own set of rules and standards and have ignored the dicta of their colleagues in other branches of bibliography. No matter how slight one's acquaintance with the standard incunabula bibliographies may be, it is no doubt apparent to everyone that incunabulists have blithely over-ruled all the elaborate regulations for describing books laid down by the American Library Association and kindred organizations. The wisdom of this – or the lack of it – is not for me to judge, but it is a fact which cannot be overlooked.'[1] Dr Bühler went on to say that the British Museum's own cataloguing rules differed from those applied to the Museum's own catalogue of incunabula and that the cataloguing rules of the Bodleian Library are not practical for describing fifteenth-century books. At first hearing, this would seem to indicate an alarming incidence of 'elephantoidal roguery' among bibliographers and librarians. It may equally be that we are hoping or striving for standardization applied to articles which are so different as to make it undesirable if not impracticable. The old 1908 cataloguing rules of the American Library Association and the (British) Library Association could never have served for cataloguing incunabula and, in view of the advances made in the last half-century in the study of incunabula, could never have been successfully adapted since that time. It is equally true to say

[1] BUHLER, Curt F., McMANAWAY, James G. *and* WROTH, Lawrence C. *Standards of Bibliographical Description.* 1949. pp. 3–4. (hereafter referred to as: *Standards of Bibliographical Description.*)

that the new rules, published in 1967, which will perhaps replace the 1908 code, are equally unsuitable. Indeed, each of the
two participating associations published separate proposals for
the cataloguing of incunabula; the Library Association compilation by Henry Guppy in 1932 and the American Library
Association by Paul Dunkin in 1951.[1] Each of these, and
particularly Paul Dunkin's, was more in the nature of a discussion than a formulation of rules. The bibliographer and the
cataloguing librarian are unlikely to be surprised by this state
of affairs. He knows that even with an agreed code of practice
for the past sixty years libraries have felt a need, real or
imaginery, for divergences from the common code. If this is so
in the case of modern books which are rarely of bibliographical
complexity, then individuality of action is all the more likely
with older books of greater bibliographical consequence.

The most massive, and to many readers the most formidable,
exposition of the problems and methodology of bibliographical
description is that set forth by Fredson Bowers in 1949.[2] It
remains the most detailed survey of the problems and it is
probably true to say that its full impact has not yet been realized.
It was so minute in its exposition and so demanding in its
requirements for bibliographical work that it was believed by
some to represent an unattainable ideal. This was, in fact, never
a danger of this book. Bibliographical work should strive for
that particular kind of perfection to which Fredson Bowers has
always pointed. A real danger lay in another direction. Bowers
accumulated so much evidence, garnered from so much experience, and expressed himself in such forthright and uncompromising terms that he seemed to bring down the tablets
from the mountain. His book could unfortunately be interpreted
as closing the discussion rather than opening it. If this were to
be so, then again sterile uniformity could result.

The important fact of Bowers' book can be summed up in

---

[1] *GUPPY*, Henry. *Rules for the Cataloguing of Incunabula.* 2nd. ed. 1932.
DUNKIN, Paul S. *How to Catalog a Rare Book.* 1951.
[2] *BOWERS*, Fredson. *Principles of Bibliographical Description.* 1949. (Re-issue, 1962)

his own words. 'The construction of a true bibliography, or even of an adequate descriptive catalogue, cannot be undertaken by an amateur who has read a few rules for bibliographical description and dipped into McKerrow's classic *Introduction to Bibliography*. With any difficult book the result will inevitably be an imperfect description and nothing else: an untrained writer cannot carry description to the start of textual criticism where, as for example with W. W. Greg, he can prove that the previously accepted text of *Lear* is based on a piracy without authority. Or, as with Hazen, expose the Kirgate forgeries of Strawberry Hill books and so help clarify Gray's text; or, as with Carter and Pollard, reveal the Wise forgeries.

'Behind a great bibliography like Greg's *Bibliography of the English Printed Drama to the Restoration* lie years of technical experience with books in general, years of the kind of investigation called *critical* or *analytical* bibliography, ready to be brought to bear on the present problems. The bare tools for this trade seem often unconnected with descriptive bibliography. But specific investigations into minute techniques of printing provide knowledge of printing practice which at some time can be used for purposes of textual criticism by the writer of an analytical descriptive bibliography. A specialist may devote years to analysing type faces and ornaments; he or someone else on this evidence may expose a forgery or piracy and clear a text. Study of the movement of formes through an early press may indicate whether or not an invariant forme has been proofed and may even at some time expose an otherwise securely hidden sheet cancel which affects the contents of a book. Every bibliographical study of printing has as its final justification the practical use in a textual study or descriptive bibliography of the information thus gained.'[1]

This serves to focus attention on the fact that critical rather than descriptive bibliography is the key to the whole issue. Once a book has been understood bibliographically and is

[1] *ibid.* p. 13.

capable of explanation, the description of the item does not raise major problems. In the words of Paul Dunkin, 'You can catalog almost any rare book adequately if you have an intelligent scepticism. The important thing is not so much what you do to the card as what you do to the book.' Above all else what is done within the description must be the free, but accurate, interpretation by the bibliographer of the facts which he has established from the book itself. In the words attributed to A. W. Pollard, 'It does not much matter what form you give to your bibliographical statement provided you make your intentions perfectly clear.'

It is probably easiest to appreciate the variety necessary in description by concentrating attention on books of widely separated periods and differing production backgrounds. The widest separation is between pre-1500 books and those printed after the great watershed date of 1800. Two major bibliographical catalogues exist which deal with books of these two periods and provide adequate illustration of the different qualities necessary in such cases. The British Museum's catalogue of fifteenth-century printed books and Michael Sadleir's bibliographical record of nineteenth-century fiction are so unlike in regard to the works being recorded that here is no sense of amazement or disappointment to the user in finding that the entries are so very different. Once again, there is no question of one set of descriptions being better than the other or of either being too elaborate or too detailed. They differ because of fundamental differences between the categories of book being described and a very substantial difference in the uses to which the completed bibliographical tools will be put. Sadleir's bibliography throws a great deal of new light on nineteenth-century book trade and publishing methods, for example, as distinct from the primarily major printing interest of the British Museum catalogue. Quite apart from other similarly differing aspects, this fact alone would be sufficient to set the descriptions a distance apart from each other.

It is perhaps not so readily apparent that strong subject

interests within a recorded collection will tend against any drift towards standardization. Occasionally this is caused by the fact that the subject itself brings about a major bibliographical difference in the book, the best example of which would be in the case of an atlas. When the catalogue or bibliography is itself directly concerned with the recording of a bibliographical feature, such as the catalogues of J. R. Abbey's plate books, then also the variations from any pre-conceived norm seem to be natural enough.[1]

An excellent example of the other type of problem is the *Catalogue of Botanical Books* in the Hunt Collection.[2] This is the record of a collection which has a strongly developed subject interest and this has shaped the catalogue. Above all, most botanical books, certainly the great ones, are lavishly illustrated and, therefore, the catalogue had to be designed to deal with this major bibliographical feature. It is a catalogue which attracts interest from several separate areas of study and which needed to have them all in mind. In his introduction Allan Stevenson wrote that, 'the true measure of a bibliographical catalogue lies not in a cold and static report on material objects, but rather in its incitement to study and enjoyment, the solution of problems, the urge to know books in more than one way. As the catalogue has been prepared for botanists first, but also for students of the art of the colorplate, and for all bibliophiles and bibliographers, each of these kinds of reader-users may find some pleasure in looking over the fence, circumspectly, to see what tall and interesting plants grow in adjacent gardens.'[3] By

[1] *Scenery of Great Britain and Ireland in Aquatint and Lithography, 1770–1860, from the library of J. R. Abbey. A bibliographical catalogue.* 1952.

Life in England in Aquatint and Lithography. 1770–1860, from the library of J. R. Abbey. A bibliographical catalogue. 1953.

Travel in Aquatint and Lithography, 1770–1860, from the library of J. R. Abbey. A bibliographical catalogue. 2 vols. 1956.

[2] *Catalogue of Botanical Books in the collection of Rachel McMasters Miller Hunt.* Hunt Foundation, Pittsburgh, Pa. 3 vols. 1961.

[3] Stevenson's introduction entitled, 'A bibliographical method for the description of botanical books' is in volume 2 of the Hunt Catalogue, pp. cxli – ccxxxi.

the time that Allan Stevenson wrote his introduction in September 1960, there were several notable publications to give inspiration and provide example. A study of the introduction, followed by use and consideration of the catalogue itself, will indicate the extent to which these examples could be followed and the measure of departure from them. It will also stress the variations from previously accepted practice which have been necessitated by the advances in bibliographical studies. Stevenson's introduction also contained these words. 'A bibliographical catalogue is an annotated or descriptive report on the individual copies of books in a library or collection of books. It is not, strictly speaking, a bibliography, for it deals mainly with single copies. But it uses bibliographical procedures and supplies material toward the making of bibliographies. The Hunt Botanical Catalogue is thus an attempt to provide accurate and informative descriptions of the books in one library. It recognizes that important botanical books of the past combine the art of the flower painter with the science of the botanist. And so the Catalogue addresses itself to a varied audience: collectors; librarians; students of nature, botany, and art; botanists; bibliographers.

'The volume devoted to eighteenth-century botanical books attempts to use those methods of transcription, collation, and description which embody the best experience of bibliographers. The system is mainly that of the Bibliographical Society, as developed and employed by Sir Walter Greg and as codified by Fredson Bowers. It now extends itself into the sciences, and adapts itself to the description of botanical works with plates, often issued by parts, in folio or broadsheet.

'In certain other respects the treatment and the content of the descriptions are new. A way has been found to include not only descriptions of full length but some shorter annotated entries for less important books and for recent accessions. The length of the full descriptions is dictated largely by the need of providing sufficient detail for the recognition of other copies in the same edition, issue, or state, even when title-pages or preliminaries are missing. Certain parts of the description are due to the growth of information on press figures, botanical plates, paper, and type. This is probably the first bibliographical catalogue to offer systematic notes of the formats, provenances, and marks of the paper on which the books are written or printed. It proposes a method for collating and listing botanical plates, a method which grows equally and naturally out of the bibliographical system used for the letterpress and the nomenclature system used by botanists. It similarly offers ways of collating broadsheet books and 'number' books, in which form many botanical works were issued. It searches for a short and useful way of listing press figures, those 'mysterious' numbers and symbols which appear (in addition to the gathering-signatures) at the foot of type-pages in English books of the eighteenth century. It records the body-type and other main types used in each book, by size-name and the measure of ten lines in millimeters. These elements of bibliographical description have been developing in the years since the Church, the Pforzheimer, and the Abbey catalogues were compiled. I hope that the newer procedures will prove useful to bibliographers searching for individual models and a forward-looking method. They will see that bibliographical method continues to develop and that the millenium is not yet.'[1]

There are many interesting features in this catalogue to which Stevenson draws attention in this introduction. First, a varying amount of detail is given for entries within this one collection; some have full descriptions, some abridged descriptions and some short. In this connection, Stevenson expresses the view that 'patterns in book description can be tyrannous'. The reasons for the variations in the treatment of detail might appear to violate a purely bibliographical principle in that they are based on the respective importance of the items. It was decided from the outset that some works merited 'less space and a simpler treatment' than others. This harks back to Pollard's

[1] *ibid.* pp. cxlii–cxliii.

contention that only a chemist could select and organize a list of books on chemistry. In the case of the Hunt Catalogue there is in addition to the general interest of a wide variety of readers, a particular interest for certain subject specialists. It is, wrote Stevenson, 'a bibliographical catalogue for the use of scientists'; because of this the needs and interests of specialist users can take precedence on occasions over purely bibliographical considerations.

The descriptions also departed from the traditional and text-book approach to the entry in the number, order and content of the parts of the description. Ten parts were identified although this number was not used invariably, even in the full descriptions. The parts were as follows:

1. Short entry; author, title, facts of publication, format
2. Transcript of title-pages
3. Collation of letterpress, with list of contents
4. List of press figures, (if any)
5. Collation of plates, (if any)
6. Note on paper; its size, source, prevailing marks, leaf size
7. Note on type; showing font and measurement of body types
8. Note on binding; with marks of provenance (if any)
9. References; bibliographies, catalogues, further copies
10. Notes, biographical, critical, botanical, bibliographical

The important variations here are those which are concerned with aspects of the book of which the real bibliographical importance has only been established in recent years. This applies with particular force to the attention given to press figures and to the evidence of paper.

When McKerrow wrote his *Introduction* he made scant mention of press figures and, indeed, committed himself to stating that the practice was 'seldom of much bibliographical importance'. This opinion was perfectly justified in the light of the evidence available in 1927. By now, opinion has changed sufficiently, in view of the work which has been done, for press figures to occupy a major and undisputed place of importance in a bibliographical catalogue. It would not be appropriate to list them as an element in all descriptions since they are applicable only to English books between the latter part of the seventeenth century and the first quarter of the nineteenth. Within these limits they are now an important part of the evidence contributed by the book which comes forward for the consideration of the bibliographer.

Paper is the most substantial single element in the book and its bibliographical importance shows itself likely to achieve a commensurate status. An important corpus of research material has been assembled during recent years and a number of bibliographical problems have yielded to the testimony. The facts are there but they are used all to infrequently in descriptive work. In Stevenson's words, 'It is obvious that the description of a book should take some notice of the type used to print it and the paper that receives the impress of that type. These are physical features as tangible as the binding and even more essential to the making of a book. Nevertheless most cataloguers and bibliographers ignore them or pass over them lightly, even when they find space to record (glowingly) the presence of original wrappers, crushed levant, or a dust-jacket.' It is right and natural that he should express this viewpoint since no individual bibliographer has done more in the last few decades than Stevenson to demonstrate the bibliographical importance of paper evidence.

Thus far, the argument has been designed to support a proposition that any attempt to impose over much standardization in bibliographical description could only work to the disadvantage of the bibliographer and of the user. There is, however, one area in which standardization could be of advantage.

Bibliography has created, or accumulated, a considerable vocabulary which needs to be used with precision but which frequently is not. Certain terms are quite basic to our understanding of the very nature of bibliographical evidence. The further our investigations are pursued, the clearer it becomes that, because of modern standards of bibliographical work, exactness is a matter of urgent importance. In the days of a more leisurely, bibliophilic attitude to bibliographical problems, possible confusions between, for example, the terms 'edition' and 'impression' did not raise any alarming difficulties. Until comparatively recent years the analysis of books had not been sufficiently detailed to permit of any subtle distinctions between 'states' and 'issues', nor the accumulation of evidence to point to their importance. Greg's 1955 Lyell Lectures considered in some detail the exact implication of terms which have a very wide and general bibliographical currency; 'licence', 'entrance', 'imprint', 'copyright'.[1] In examples such as these, and in many more besides, it can be said that, until they have been fully understood and are always used with accuracy and clarity, no bibliographical description, however rudimentary, can be relied upon implicitly.

It will have become apparent by now that a complete biblio-graphical appreciation of the book is the most important element in description. Once the book has been analysed and understood; the particular function of the list, catalogue, or bibliography agreed upon; then the description has a good chance of being effective. In fact, it could be said that analytical bibliography is the most important part of descriptive work. Nevertheless, it should not be assumed that the technique of the description itself does not raise many issues. The majority of these problems are primarily factual and are dealt with in the manuals and discussions on description such as Bowers, Cowley, Dunkin, Esdaile, McKerrow and Stevenson. There is however, one special aspect of description which has been widely ventilated in recent years but where the opposing view-points are still as widely separated as ever.

Within the description itself, the first and most obvious part is invariably the transcript of the title-page. This has been the

[1] *GREG*, W. W. *Some Aspects and Problems of London Publishing between 1550 and 1650.* 1956.

major element in descriptive bibliography ever since its beginnings. No major disputes have ever raged over the details of a transcript although many bibliographers have adopted an individual approach designed to meet the problems of a particular book or of one particular period and especially so with reference to type used on the title-page. The larger dispute has arisen over a matter of general principle. Many transcripts of title-pages have to deal with intricate problems of type layout, various type designs and sizes, and of ornamentation. The problem is particularly apparent when the title-page is distinguished by some over-riding feature of which no representative symbols are possible, yet upon which much depends. For example, a sixteenth-century title-page with a wood-cut border raises problems of this kind. The fact that the quasi-facsimile description in such instances can refer to a full description in a bibliography or catalogue of title-page borders is not a solution of the problem, it has simply transferred it on to other shoulders. Yet in such cases an attempt can be made because there is a typographical element within the border. The problem becomes much more difficult with engraved title-pages. Each one becomes more individual and the opportunity to refer to an element common to two or more title-pages, as with wood-cut borders, is no longer possible. When such engraved title-pages defy any normal attempt at description and, additionally, are of historic or artistic merit as with a title-page of William Blake, then the problem becomes acute. Because of these difficulties, suggestions have frequently been made that a photo facsimile of the title-page should serve instead of the quasi-facsimile transcript.

The proposal is not a new one. At the International Conference of Librarians held in London in 1877 Henry Stevens, the great Anglo-American bookseller, read a paper entitled *Photo-Bibliography*. His suggestions included one for a bibliographical bureau for the cataloguing of books of importance and the issuing of the description in printed form. In the case of books with title-pages which were not amenable to normal procedures of transcription Stevens proposed the addition to the transcription of a photographic reproduction of the title-page. Although opinions at the time were mixed, opposition appears to have been chiefly on the grounds of expense. One major catalogue which did make use of this idea to a limited extent was George Watson Cole's catalogue of the Church collection in 1907. For a long time it was only the economics of production which was urged against the method and as eminent a bibliographer as Lawrence Wroth in a chapter on 'Early Americana' could recommend as a standard, 'Photographic reproduction of title-page, if possible, but if not, full or adequate transcription of title and imprint . . .'[1] Of recent years, however, more stringent objections have been raised.

The arguments which have been raised against this proposed solution are many and have been most forcibly stated by Fredson Bowers. The most spirited defence of photographic reproduction has been by Philip Gaskell in his letter in the *Transactions of the Bibliographical Society*.[2] The primary objection is usually that anything which relies on photography is open to all the usual objections to photographic work, above all that it can be inaccurate. There are always dire warnings as to what *can* happen and examples of what *has* happened. In Bowers' words, 'A flyspeck was the source of a long-standing misreading in a reproduction of a Shakespeare Folio.' The counter that this is a limitation which can be removed by careful proof-reading (the responsibility of the bibliographer rather than the block-maker) raises the whole question of standards of photographic work with, again, the problems of cost, Even some expensive and apparently scholarly photo-facsimile publications can be faulted on their standards of accurate recording. A second objection is that much bibliographical work, even at second hand, requires an accuracy which is beyond the capabilities of many of the usual methods of photographic reproduction. Line-block work would be chosen more than any other process

[1] *Standards of Bibliographical Description*. p. 117.
[2] *The Library*: Fifth Series. Vol. VII (1952), pp. 135–137.

because of its economy, but it is a process which is unreliable as a means of conveying the accurate detail of a title-page. There is no adequate way of controlling the extent of the bite of the acid on the plate and it is this which determines the actual print on the paper itself. On the other hand Gaskell wrote that, 'A good craftsman can do almost anything with a line-block, and provided that the bibliographer will tell him exactly what is required, he can make a thoroughly faithful reproduction every time.' At the other end of the scale, collotype would give the most accurate representation of any, although still not perfect, but the price would be unrealistic to the purpose of many bibliographies and catalogues and there would be an undue limitation upon the number of copies available. In between these extremes, half-tone, gravure and lithography represent a sliding scale of cost, accuracy and general availability.

Two possible compromises appear to be worthy of consideration. The first is to use photo-facsimile only as an addition to quasi-facsimile transcription and, therefore, not to allow the effect of the description to depend upon it entirely. Above all else this permits the bibliographer to utilize it only in those instances where pictorial representation seems to make a very real contribution to the objectives of the description. The second is almost a variation of the first and that is to use photography, not necessarily for the whole title-page, but for those elements which need that particular kind of emphasis. For example, signatures or marks of ownership which appear on title-pages, or elsewhere, and which are of considerable importance in determining provenance of copies, or manuscript press-marks for the same purpose, printer's marks and ornaments, could well be supplied in facsimile.

In the last resort there can be only one criterion. The purpose of the title-page description is to set the detail of the page as clearly and as accurately as possible before the reader. At its very highest level it should enable the user to have as distinct an impression as he would have with the page itself before him.

Taking into account such considerations of cost and use as should apply, then the method of transcription used should be that which most nearly attains to this objective. The same kind of assessment has to be made in relation to the overall purpose of the whole description. Recent bibliographical work has demonstrated more and more the individuality of the copy and thus has given more pointers to the detail in which this individuality should be defined in the description. The item which, during many years of instruction in bibliographical description, read quite simply as 'facts relating to this particular copy' has now to be reinterpreted. The limit in the past was largely to matters such as tears, imperfections, stains, marks of ownership, manuscript notes, binding and so on. They were all matters concerned with the condition of the copy on the assumption that the state would be identical between copies, Now, when it becomes necessary to particularize a copy, as for example in a library catalogue, then these marks of individuality within the main body of the book must be made clear.

5
Arrangement
of a
bibliography

The function of a bibliography of any type, enumerative or descriptive, can never be fully realized unless the method chosen to display the material is really adequate. There are many examples of excellent listings of titles which are made thoroughly ineffective by the method of arrangement. The problem is found in major bibliographies, where it can be a severe limitation on the usefulness of an otherwise painstaking work, and is also found in selective reading lists appended to the chapters of a book under the misleading and erroneous heading of 'bibliography'.

Although it cannot be regarded as an activity which represents a major function of the bibliographer it is one which reflects directly on his work. The term systematic bibliography has frequently been used as a synonym for what is more generally called enumerative bibliography. It is really in this area of the arrangement of the material that the fundamental idea of a systemization can be found. Also although it is most generally applied to the construction of an enumerative bibliography, precisely the same task faces the descriptive bibliographer. The material must be ordered if it is to serve any purpose other than that of a purely preservative record. It is a function which has much in common with the ordering, arrangement and indexing of material within a book. Many possible methods could be selected which would be appropriate in certain special circumstances, but the claims for particular attention can be argued in the instances of the three most general bases for arrangement; alphabetical, chronological and subject.

Alphabetical Arrangement

An alphabetical arrangement is the one which frequently suggests itself as being relatively uncomplicated and comprehensible by all users. Half a century ago Pollard used these arguments and wrote, 'If we may take anything at all for granted on the part of our readers we may assume a knowledge of the alphabet. The principle of arrangement will be continuously visible. Abrahams will succeed Abbott, and Acheson succeed Abrahams in the most obvious sequence possible. Moreover, unless the phoneticians have their way and provide the English language with an entirely new set of symbols – which is improbable – the sequence of the letters of the alphabet is not likely to be altered. Our method of arrangement will be as good twenty years hence as on the day when our work was done.'[1] Against these positive advantages the only limitation which Pollard could see to put upon its use was simply that it gave little or no help to the reader

In the light of fuller consideration other problems arise to dampen this optimism. Although the alphabet is well known and easily recognized, the rules of alphabetization are far more complicated. The basic question is the decision as to whether the letters of the words being arranged shall be organized on the 'word by word' or 'the nothing before something' principle as contrasted with the 'letter by letter' or 'all-through' arrangement. If the former then the arrangement would be:

> New Amsterdam
> New England
> New wives for old
> Newark
> Newman

[1] *The Library*: Second Series: Vol. X (1909). pp. 871–87. (reprinted by Association of Assistant Librarians. London. 1950).

If the arrangement is the 'all-through' principle the result would be:

> New Amsterdam
> Newark
> New England
> Newman
> New wives for old

In a letter to S. W. Lawley in October 1882, Henry Bradshaw wrote that this 'is what I call the Sanskrit plan, by which all the words are run together and treated as one'; 'I know', he wrote, 'it is adopted by many great authorities and by many practical people; for my own part I cannot see it.' By its nature, Bradshaw saw that the all-through principle must also separate entries which, although not alike, have at least some kinship. 'We had a great discussion last term about it on the Library Syndicate, Luard and others strongly advocating your plan. But today somebody wanted an Arabic writer *Ali* something or other, and we found in the catalogue that Ali Baba was separated from Ali Musa by a lot of Aliberts, Alienus, etc., groups of Ali . . . then names like Alison, then more Ali's and so on, until it was quite bewildering.'[1]

It is difficult, almost impossible, to urge that one is more easily understood than the other; both are straightforward alphabetical arrangements, but strongly expressed views can be found supporting either far wing of the disputation. From the viewpoint of the compiler the important factor is consistency; whichever one is chosen must be adhered to completely. From the user's standpoint, although either is comprehensible, it is necessary to know which one has been chosen in order to use the compilation. Other decisions, all affecting consistency, cover matters such as the treatment of 'Mc' and 'Mac', of the 'O'' surnames and of prefixes in general.

With the growth of world bibliography, and especially with

[1] *Fasciculus Ioanni Willis Clark Dicatus*. Cambridge University Press, 1099. pp. 132-133.

an increasing bibliographical interest in countries which have non-Roman alphabets, problems which had hitherto arisen largely in connection with mixed languages occur more frequently for mixed alphabets. Rules for the transliteration or romanization of alphabets have existed from the early days of bibliography and catalogue compilation but now their use is becoming increasingly common. One of the best recent examples of the arrangements of titles covering various languages, including those which need transliteration, is the *World List of Scientific Periodicals*.

The danger which Pollard saw of the linguists' providing the language with a new set of symbols is now more real than when he wrote. Although the experiments in new alphabets are for specialized purposes only, and are unlikely to affect the alphabetical order of major bibliographies as things now are, the sense of permanency of the old order has been shaken and change is now more likely than for several centuries.

In spite of the fact that alphabetical order seems so logical and so easy to comprehend it is clear that peculiar difficulties can arise even in these cases. The biggest drawback, however, is the one which Pollard mentioned originally, the unrevealing nature of alphabetical order and the lack of assistance which is afforded to a subject inquiry. It has the utility of an index but cannot provide a service beyond that point. Its main function, therefore, is in instances where there is no logical order of the parts, such as in cases of author or title, and most usually as a secondary form of arrangement, since the primary one has frequently to be subject. It is also true that its disadvantages appear less obviously when the entry is relatively limited in scope and the basis of the arrangement is more clearly visible.

The S.T.C. provides an example of a bibliography in which alphabetical order provides an obvious answer. Material of this nature is required far less from the subject standpoint and the main purpose is primarily for the identification of the individual titles. It is the use which the bibliographer expects to be made of such material which leads to the arrangement in this particular instance. The same titles can be – and it is hoped will sometimes be – arranged in a different order to achieve a different purpose. Other factors which are of equal concern in a bibliography such as the S.T.C., where the emphasis is on the 'book-trade' aspects of the entries, are for the identification of printer, publisher and bookseller. These have now been covered by the separately published index by Paul Morrison of these features. Between them these features cover the main likely approaches to the material. The one remaining aspect of importance is the chronological one.

Chronological Arrangement

Ever since the original publication of the S.T.C., the Biblio-graphical Society has realized the importance of a chronological arrangement of the material as an ultimate objective. In a bibliography such as this, of primarily historical material, chronological arrangement can reveal aspects of growth and relationship between items which would otherwise not be apparent. This is one of the criteria by which an arrangement should be judged; namely, that it should be more than a simple aid to retrieval. It must in addition add significantly to the basic information by the creation of linkages and juxtapositions. Chronological order is frequently the one to do this in marked degree. Whenever the development of the material needs to be demonstrated its advantages can fruitfully be argued. The chronological editing, or re-arrangement, of the S.T.C. is ten-tatively entitled the *Annals of English Printing* and, on its publi-cation, it will be possible to trace the development of English printing year by year. As the S.T.C. itself was the starting point for so much bibliographical work, so, it can be anticipated, will the *Annals* be equally important. The only major chronological guides to any areas of England printing at present are the contemporary ones, such as the *Transcript of the Registers of the Company of Stationers* and the *Term Catalogues*.[1] In spite of their

[1] Stationers' Company. *Transcript of the Registers of the Company* ... *1554–1640*, edited by Edward Arber. 5 vols. 1874–1894. *continued* for 1641–1708, edited by

limited coverage and the imperfections to be expected of this kind of compilation, they provide important source material, but much more is needed.

The revelation of the growth of a subject or of a literary or bibliographical form, when the material is arranged chronologically, can also be seen in one of this century's outstanding bibliographies. When Greg came to consider the arrangement for his *Bibliography of the English Printed Drama to the Restoration* he considered the possiblities of arrangement by author, by title or by date. The first loses much of its validity in this particular instance because of the large proportion of works of uncertain authorship. The second is relatively clear but is uninformative. The third, upon which he finally decided, is, when equipped with full indexes, remarkably easy to use. It also demonstrates, with remarkable clarity, the development of English drama during this period and thereby adds an extra dimension to bibliography.

One disadvantage which may occur to some users is that chronological order has never been utilized by any major classification scheme as a main basis of book arrangement. Although this should not necessarily militate against its use in a bibliography, some users wish to see a direct relationship between the sequence in a bibliography and on the shelves of a library. Although it would never be suggested that a bibliography should be so closely allied to a shelf order as to become virtually a catalogue, there is one instance where this relationship exists.

When Proctor produced the *Index to the Early Printed Books in the British Museum* he adopted the arrangement discussed by Bradshaw and based on his 'natural history' order.[1] At the time

---

G. E. B. Eyre, transcribed by H. R. Plomer. 3 vols. 1913–1914.

ARBER, Edward. *The Term Catalogues, 1668–1709*, with a number for Easter term, 1711. 3 vols. 1903–1906.

[1] *PROCTOR*, Robert. *Index to the Early Printed Books in the British Museum . . . to 1500, with notes of those in the Bodleian Library.* 4. vols. 1898–1899.

when Proctor used this it was not a form of arrangement adopted by any major library. In his preface to the work he argued in favour of this arrangement:

'As the chief object of a list of this kind is to illustrate the early history of printing, the arrangement adopted is not that by authors' names (like that of Hain), but chronological, similar to that of Panzer, with modifications. It is that sanctioned by the highest modern authorities in this branch of bibliography, J. W. Holtrop and Henry Bradshaw. It may be called the historical method, as it aims at following as closely as it is possible consistently with clearness the developments of printing in the various countries and towns in which it was practised in the fifteenth century. No other arrangement suitable for use on a large scale shows in the same way the inter-relation of different presses, and the transference of types from one printer to another. Panzer's method of grouping of books by years rather than by printers has many merits, but obscures the work of the individual printers, and is unsuitable to a work in which the chief stress is laid on this point, and on the types which the printers used.'

This work makes an interesting comparison, from the viewpoint of chronological arrangement, with Greg's bibliography. Whereas the latter is one simple chronological sequence, Proctor's *Index* was arranged on a more complex plan. In the preface he went on to write: 'They (the books) are arranged, mainly in chronological order, under the printers of them; the printers are arranged in their order under the towns, and the towns under the countries; the precedence assigned to countries, towns and printers is the same in principle, and is determined by the *terminus a quo* in point of date, in each case.' This bibliography provides as good an example as possible of chronological order applied to the fullest possible extent. It exhibits all the advantages of the scheme, and in particular the variety of aspects of early printing which arise from the arrangement.

Although it can be objected that the *Index* is more specifically a catalogue than a pure bibliography, the objection ceases to have force when the arrangement is the point at issue. The same organization would be the ideal for a bibliography of early printing. So much has the arrangement proved itself that it has increasingly become the popular method of arrangement for the books themselves. By 1908 when the first volume of the British Museum's *Catalogue of Books Printed in the XVth Century* appeared Pollard was able to write in his 'Introduction' that the experience of Proctor with his *Index* had made this the obvious arrangement for a much larger catalogue. The XVth century catalogue is currently the most important single tool of its kind and affects profoundly the world-wide study of incunabula. It should not be forgotten how much of its importance depends on the arrangement. In this particular instance the arrangement, developed by a number of noted incunabulists and finally used by Proctor, has laid down the main approach to the study for the past half-century.

It is not only in instances of older books that such a chronological order may serve. For bibliographies of modern books it may well be the most revealing also. It is so in such an overall conspectus as Charles Evans' *American Bibliography* which gives an annual listing of American imprints from 1639 to 1800.[1] This provides exactly the kind of guidance as the Bibliographical Society's *Annals of English Printing* plans to do for English books. On a more restricted scale so far as coverage is concerned, but with correspondingly increased bibliographical detail is Philip Gaskell's *Bibliography of the Foulis Press*.[2]

It is equally applicable as either a main or subsidiary arrangement in the case of personal bibliographies. In its most elementary form it can be a perfectly straightforward chronological listing as in R. W. Chapman's *Jane Austen*.[3] This is the simplest of all cases because it dealt with an author of limited output working entirely within one literary form. The same kind of pattern emerges, but with a larger bibliographical panoply, in

[1] *EVANS*, Charles. *American Bibliography*. 14 vols. 1903–1959.
[2] *GASKELL*, Philip. *A Bibliography of the Foulis Press*. 1964.
[3] *CHAPMAN*, R. W. *Jane Austen. A critical bibliography*. 1953.

Sir Geoffrey Keynes' *Bibliography of William Harvey*.[1] Here the three main works, exclusive of collected editions and miscellanea, are arranged by date of first publication: *De motu cordis* (1628); *De circulatione sanguinis* (1649); *De generatione animalium* (1651). Within the section for each book the successive printings and editions are arranged in chronological order.

A slight variation of this pattern is introduced into the bibliographies of certain authors when the primary arrangement is by kind of material with date of publication used as a secondary arrangement. Thus, in Warren Roberts' *Bibliography of D. H. Lawrence*, the main division is into (a) books and pamphlets, (b) contributions to books, (c) contributions to periodicals, (d) translations.[2] These are followed by two supplementary sections on his manuscripts and the books and pamphlets relating to D. H. Lawrence. Within each category date of original publication dictates the order. Since 'first editions' only are listed there is no real complication with dates running on for later printings apart from the listing of 'American first editions'. This means, for example, that the first edition of *Love Among the Haystacks* (1930) is separated from the first edition of his following book *Apocalypse* (1931) by the 'first American edition' of *Love Among the Haystacks* (1933).

Chronology, therefore, may be expected as a part of the scheme of arrangement in many instances. So far as printed material is concerned it is particularly significant as a basis for arrangement since few facts about a work exceed in importance the place of its publication in the order of an author's writings, and the sequence of its various printings.

Subject Arrangements

In a vast number of instances the primary interest of a book is its subject matter. It follows naturally that the most useful arrangement in such circumstances is a subject one. When this decision has been taken the major problem still remains, to

[1] *KEYNES*, Sir Geoffrey. *Bibliography of William Harvey*. 2nd ed. 1953.
[2] *ROBERTS*, Warren. *A Bibliography of D. H. Lawrence*. 1963.

determine the basis on which the subject groupings shall be organized.

The cardinal point for emphasis is that arrangement cannot be fully determined until the material has been assembled. There is an idea prevalent in the minds of some people that it is possible to determine the order relating to a particular subject field in ignorance of what quantity or type of material might be amassed. The idea is possibly widespread among librarians because of their knowledge of classification schemes. The fact that it has been found possible to construct, with varying degrees of success, a comprehensive classification of all human knowledge encourages the belief that this would be suited to the purposes of a bibliography. The differences, however, are profound and important. Material should be collected and the order established in the light of that experience and based on a close knowledge of the collection.

The major book classification schemes which have been published cover the whole range of human knowledge and in no instance is one detailed enough to reveal the more intricate relationships of a bibliography. As more precise and more detailed classifications are established in narrower subject fields there is an increasing possiblity that some of these could serve as the foundation for a bibliographical scheme. There seems to be little purpose served in forcing a bibliography into some Procrustean bed without real cause. The most potent cause is when there is a wish to ally the bibliography to a specific collection of books, in which case the bibliography begins to take on some of the characteristics of a printed catalogue.

When A. W. Pollard wrote his short paper on 'The arrangement of bibliographies' he accepted the one over-riding advantage of the Dewey Decimal Classification Scheme by saying, 'It can be worked.' He then went on, 'But to apply the decimal classification to bibliographies is monstrous and ridiculous. We are no longer dealing with titles which represent individual copies of the books, placed on certain shelves in one library, to which the reader of the catalogue can go. We are dealing with the titles merely as records of what has been written on the subject, and our one object must now be to exhibit the literature and its subdivisions as clearly and as simply as possible. Now there is no natural law that every subject must be divisible by ten, and to insist on dividing every subject in this way is absurd. As long as we are dealing with a subject of which we are ignorant the absurdity, of course, does not strike us very emphatically. But as soon as we know a subject and contrast any decimal classification of it with a natural arrangement of the headings by a man who has really studied the literature, then the absurdity is revealed.

'In the first volume of the New series of *The Library* (pp. 368–372) Mr Weale propounded an arrangement suitable for a bibliography of books about architecture, let anyone who knows anything about architecture contrast the scheme with any decimal classification of the subject and its superior reasonableness will at once be evident.

'M. Léopold Delisle has instanced liturgiology as another heading which any decimal classification reduces to chaos. The heading "Liturgies" in the British Museum catalogue was arranged in consultation by Mr Proctor and Mr Henry Jenner, who has studied liturgies all his life. Compare the scheme of this again with any decimal scheme that can be devised and the superiority of the natural order will not long remain doubtful.'

It was only the historical accident of the time of Pollard's writing which limited his strictures to a decimal classification. Later schemes and newly emerging principles, although removing some major defects, have still not produced schemes which would be suited to this particular usage. The main benefit derived from any formal classification scheme used in this connection would lie in having a closely subdivided analysis of the field. The point which Pollard made regarding architecture and liturgies raises another important issue. The compiler of a bibliography needs foremost to be a specialist in that subject field rather than primarily a bibliographer. His specialization will begin to show in particular when he comes to the detail of arrangement. It is, as Pollard suggested, utterly impossible for the non-specialist to perform usefully in this area. In some areas of detailed work, such as the layout of the entry itself, he may need the assistance of the bibliographer, or preferably combine both functions in himself; but the subject knowledge is paramount.

In spite of all the known difficulties, and chiefly because of the very real demand by book users for such tools, subject bibliographies arranged in subject order continue to be compiled. An investigation of some of them would help to identify the problems and establish such principles as are valid. This chapter, however, is not designed to deal with the problems of bibliography compilation and arrangement, but rather to specify what problems the bibliographer has to face as a part of his trade so that his whole function may be more evident.

6

Textual bibliography

This is currently the most controversial area of bibliography; primarily it is so because here it impinges upon the other disciplines which it sets out to serve. These other disciplines are old and have become extremely settled in their ways, consequently there has been a tendency to resent the intrusive gambits of the newcomer. Literary criticism and textual editing are the two fields most affected by textual bibliography and fresh confrontations appear with stringent regularity.

In essence, textual bibliography works on the theory that some understanding of the physical processes which result in the publication and dissemination of a book can, in certain circumstances, have a bearing on the development of the text. The text is carried by the process of printing and a study of textual bibliography will provide evidence that the bibliographical analysis of the book can sometimes most fully illuminate the text.

A simple non-bibliographical example will demonstrate this. An old style Christmas party game was that of 'passing the message'. A number of people were seated in a line, the first one whispered a message into the ear of the second who, in turn whispered it to the third. In time the message reached the end of the line and it could be seen, or heard, how the text had changed in the course of its passage. Normally the laughter which greeted the mutilated text ended the whole of the exercise. It would, however, be possible on any occasion such as this, and probably enlightening, to try and establish how the changes had crept in. It would be necessary to ask each individual to recall how he received the message and how he passed it on. Attention would have to be paid to certain physical characteristics of each participant. The fact that one was deaf, that another had a speech impediment, that another spoke in an unfamiliar accent, that one was a party wag who substituted for the fun of it: these are circumstances which could have caused corruptions. Such corruptions could only be unravelled in the light of the physical attributes of the individual members, each of which would affect the understanding of the problems of the text in a different way.

A book passes through a similar set of circumstances during its production.

As bibliographical studies developed in the later decades of the nineteenth century a few bibliographers began to pay attention to this aspect. The turning point came with the work which Pollard and Greg did on the '1619' quartos. It was not only that the work itself was of such outstanding importance but also that their example and, to some extent, their direct teaching encouraged others to apply themselves to similar studies.

Following closely upon these important bibliographical events the first real attempt to assess the new position was made when Greg delivered the Sandars Lectures at Cambridge in 1913. He chose as his theme 'Bibliographical and textual problems of the English miracle plays' and in the course of these lectures he made some general observations on the role of bibliography.[1]

In the first of these lectures, Greg said, 'The importance of bibliography for the study of literature is sometimes forgotten alike by the bibliographer and the critic. The former immerses himself in subjects which, however interesting in themselves,

---

[1] *The Library*: Third Series: Vol V (1914) pp. 1–30; 168–205; 280–319; 365–399.
Also issued in pamphlet form, A. Moring. London. 1914.

lead to few developments beyond their own horizon: the latter is habitually shy of investigations in a region in which he feels he is not at home. It is well, therefore, occasionally, to insist on the connection between the two provinces, and to show how intimate it is by attending to some of the problems that lie along the border.' In fact Greg was to spend the rest of his long life insisting on this connection and 'attending to some of the problems'. This relationship he demonstrated more fully in relation to the drama than to anything else but of this part of his work he was able to say in his 1913 lectures. '. . . I hope before I have done to show how impossible it is to treat at all adequately the literary problems of the early drama without at every turn having recourse to what a friend of mine has recently styled the "higher bibliography".'

This was a forthright claim but one which Greg was able to substantiate throughout the course of his Sandars lectures and, subsequently, in his life's work. In retrospect, however, the clearest and most uncompromising statement which Greg was ever to make was in the paper entitled 'What is bibliography?', which he read to the Bibliographical Society on 19th February 1912.[1] If disagreements have since arisen as to the function and importance of bibliography it is important to look back to this clear exposition to which few people would now take exception. Greg opened by drawing attention to the changing status of bibliography, a change which had been largely effected by the work which he, together with Pollard and McKerrow, had done since the beginning of the century.

'It is a commonplace among those who have written on the subject, that bibliography has grown from being an art into being a science, and if we are content not to press the terms too closely, the remark may be accepted as indicating a certain truth. There was a time not so long ago when the typical occupation of bibliographers was the writing of elegant essays on individual points of archaeological or artistic interest, more or

---

[1] *Transactions of the Bibliographical Society.* Vol. xii (1914). pp. 39–53.

less closely, and more or less accidentally, connected with books. It is no reproach to a generation of book-lovers, many of whom are fortunately still active in our midst, that this should have been so. If bibliography is to-day a science by which we co-ordinate facts and trace the operation of constant causes, if we are gradually evolving a rigorous method for the investigation and interpretation of fresh evidence, if we are able, within the sphere of our work, in any way adequately to reconstruct the past out of the indications of the present, it is in a large measure due to the patient accumulation and recording of facts achieved by those bibliographical pioneers. As has happened over and over again in the history of science, these workers pursued the subject for its own interest and their individual amusement, and in doing so evolved a powerful instrument of investigation of the practical applications of which they never dreamed. All this we have inherited and our debt is great.'

He then attacked as so often in later years, any attempt to limit bibliography to the fields of systematic and descriptive bibliography although he was well aware, as might be expected of the future compiler of the greatest of descriptive bibliographies, of the basic, initial importance of this part of the study. 'But in so far as a science is merely descriptive it is sterile. You may dissect and you may describe, but until your anatomy becomes comparative you will never arrive at the principle of evolution. You may name and classify the colours of your sweet peas and produce nothing but a florists' catalogue; it is only when you begin grouping them according to their genetic origin that you will arrive at Mendel's formula.'

Greg spoke of his own experience of stumbling 'into bibliography by accident. Finding it impossible to obtain the information I required about a certain class of literature, I set to work to collect it. It was the results of bibliography that I wanted, but my search led me to the far greater discovery of the importance of the subject itself. Any value my literary work may have will be chiefly owing to that discovery. For, if I may be allowed a violent metaphor which is always coming to my mind, it is only by the application of a rigorous bibliographical method that the last drop of information can be squeezed out of a literary document.'

Then in words, the general tenor of which Greg was not to vary for the next forty-six years, he developed his main thesis of the role of bibliography as 'the handmaid of literature'.

'There is a remark in Dr Copinger's inaugural address before this Society that recently caught my attention. "Bibliography" he said "has been called the grammar of literary investigation." It is an extraordinary penetrating remark, but one which seems to me to have been strangely misunderstood. Bibliography has hardly ever attempted to be the grammar of literature: it has tried to be a dictionary. It has chronicled and described, sometimes it has even criticized, the books needed for the study of literature, and it has rendered valuable service in this line; but seldom if ever has it concerned itself with the methods of that study. By this, of course, I do not mean either the canons of criticism – if such exist – nor the methods of literary history, but I do mean what is antecedent to both these, namely the investigation of texts. Strictly bibliographical investigation forms three-fourths of textual criticism, and therefore of the work of the scientific editor. For editing should be none the less scientific because it must at the same time be literary. No editor, whatever his taste, ever did valuable work without a scientific power of handling textual evidence; just as no editor, however scientific, is worth his salt without taste. And apart from taste he requires much knowledge that has nothing to do with bibliography. He requires a thorough knowledge of linguistics and a thorough knowledge of antiquities. But these are presupposed in the subject and differ with the accidents of the subject. What is constant as a requirement, what every editor, what every textual investigator needs, what may therefore be truly called the grammar of literature, is critical bibliography. Critical bibliography is the science of the material transmission of literary texts, the investigation of the textual tradition as it is called, in so far as that investigation is possible without extraneous aids. It aims at the construction of a calculus for the determination of textual problems.

'This, of course, is no new science: editors have been forced to solve the problems as they went along, and in doing so they have necessarily evolved a method of their own. It is strange, however, when one comes to go into the subject, how little and often how unsatisfactory is the writing of a general nature thereon. I say this advisedly in spite of full knowledge of, and sincerest respect for, the profound observations for instance of Westcott and Hort in connection with the manuscripts of the Greek Testament. Everywhere the editor suffers from not being a bibliographer, he gives himself all sorts of unnecessary trouble and arrives at all sorts of impossible results. In the current number of one of the chief critical journals a writer goes hopelessly wrong over the order of two issues of a printed book, simply because he does not know how to distinguish an original leaf from a cancel. It is pathetic to find editors discussing the order of undated editions on a basis of vague probabilities, when often the erroneous retention of a catchword or some similar bibliographical trifle puts the matter altogether beyond dispute. It is not that bibliographers ought to rush into the task of editing, but that editors ought to give themselves a thorough bibliographical training. For a large part of their work is bibliography, critical bibliography, and this can only be properly executed when the elements of the subject have been mastered. For anyone without a competent knowledge of bibliography to endeavour to deal with textual evidence is mere impertinence. It is the task of bibliographers at present to systematize the knowledge acquired in this department and to perfect the method, that it may be required with the least possible trouble and applied with the greatest possible certainty. There is much to be done in this line. Too often far-reaching deductions are drawn from wholly inadequate premises, tables of relationship too often invite the sneer that they resemble figures of Euclid in which a bomb has exploded, too often sources of error are overlooked, too often consequences ignored.'

The last part of this remarkable lecture of Greg's was devoted to his 'describing a dream'. Here, having outlined the necessity for bibliographical studies as a part of literary studies, Greg outlined his proposals for a plan to bring about this closer association between the two studies.

'It is of a course of lectures on English bibliography which may one day be delivered at one of our so-called seats of learning, neither this year nor next year, but perhaps some day. And I will tell you what, as I dream, the lecturer will tell his class. He will begin with the general principles of textual transmission, which are for the most part obvious enough, how a number of steps often intervene between the work as it formed itself in the author's mind and as it reaches modern readers. He will pass on to describe the conditions under which manuscripts were written and copied, the kinds of mistake that scribes habitually made, and the manner in which bibliographical investigation may reveal them, the extent of the corruption to be expected and the degree to which it is reasonable to rely on the textual tradition. He will consider the influences to which manuscripts have been subjected, the injury they have suffered, the degree to which this can be repaired, the reagents that may be used with safety, the way vellum should be treated, and the way it should not. He will then deal with the principles of textual criticism, the groupings of manuscripts according to their genetic relations, the manner in which those relations are to be determined, and the way in which they affect the choice of readings: in what cases a reading in the archetype can be postulated with certainty, in what cases it is only a matter of probability: what evidence forces us to suppose conflation, what latitude should be allowed for coincidence: when conflation is due to the scribe, when to a reviser: how archetypal foliation may be inferred and what is its importance. He will then proceed to take individual monuments of literature and describe the manuscripts in which they are preserved and the relation of those manuscripts. He will also consider the contents of various manuscripts and the light which they may throw upon the

works contained. He will not neglect external evidence as regards the authors and their works, but will direct attention to
the main contemporary authorities and records to be studied.
Further, he will consider the appeal of the manuscripts; the
learned English manuscripts of the Anglo-Saxon times, the
popular manuscripts of the centuries following the Conquest.
Pari passu he will investigate changes in the methods of book-
making and the gradual developments of hand-writing. He will
indicate the evolution from the half-uncial of the earliest
charters to the final dissolution of Saxon writing about 1200,
and from the adoption and adaptation of the Carolingian minis-
cule to the book and current hands of the fifteenth century: he
will also trace the elaboration and decay of the system of con-
tractions borrowed from Latin writing. Naturally he will not
be able to deal fully with all the extant manuscripts of all sur-
viving works, but he will consider all the more important monuments, and will in particular devote attention to those that
present problems of a typical nature. He will discuss the so-
called three texts of the *Vision of Piers Plowman,* for if bibliography is not concerned with the question whether they are the
work of one author or of three, it is concerned with the determination and differentiation of the three types, a question the
investigation of which has been as yet only begun, but which
when answered will go far towards answering the other. Similarly he will discuss the already mentioned problem of the
order of the *Canterbury Tales,* so far as this depends for its
solution on the arrangement in the manuscripts.

'He will next pass to the introduction of printing, and indicate the differences which that event made in the transmission
of texts. He will discuss the relation of editions and their grouping, and also the minor differences which copies of the same
edition present, and he will indicate how the change from
manuscripts to printed books affects the problems of textual
criticism. He will call attention to the particular errors which
are likely to happen in composition and imposition, as he
previously did to those peculiar to copying. He will describe the

differences of type and their value in dating books, and also the particular literal confusions to which each is liable. He will consider methods of detecting false imprints and misleading dates. He will then proceed to deal with individual works, and beginning with the great compilation known as the *Morte Darthur*, will trace the fortunes of English literature as they depend on the printed page. He will call attention to the differences between various ages in the extent to which we may presume an author to have exercised control over the first edition of his work, or over the first and subsequent editions as well. He will enumerate the many small points, the corrections, the cancels, the withdrawals, that bear witness to an editorial supervision, and will discuss the relations of the author, the publisher, and the printer, the control that one had over the other, and that those in authority had over them all. He will expound the conditions of copyright and estimate the effect they had on literary production. Following in the footsteps of our Honorary Secretary he will reconstruct the history of the first folio of Shakespeare's plays from the evidence of exceptional copies and other bibliographical peculiarities, and he will explain the variants in the different issues of *Paradise Lost*. He will account for the duplicate setting of Erasmus' *Paraphrase*, and estimate the force of trades-unionism in the sixteenth century. Nor will he forget the manuscripts of a later date. He will give help in the decyphering and dating of Tudor and Stuart hands, and will discuss the most satisfactory way of printing works written in them. This is an important matter, and he will devote considerable attention throughout to various styles of editing. For there is no one method which is correct to the exclusion of others; it is a question which is best adapted to peculiar needs. And it is largely the business of the bibliographer to see that, whatever method is adopted, it is carried out consistently and made to yield the very best results of which it is capable.'

This is still an important document because, so far as this country is concerned, its main proposals are still ignored rather than disputed. Greg's own University, although possessing the oldest founded lectures on bibliography on the country, is far from accepting his doctrines officially. It is of the utmost importance to realize how frequently the possible aid of bibliography in textual studies has been ignored or flatly denied by prominent literary scholars. Their attitudes are of concern because they are precisely those whom bibliography seeks mainly to serve.

E. M. W. Tillyard, in his account of the development of English studies at Cambridge, described the battle between the 'linguistic' and 'literary' attitudes to English literature and he treated fairly harshly the 'emotional' criticism of Quiller-Couch, Stopford Brooke and Saintsbury: 'criticism mainly for the ends of gossip and praise'.[1] He also sketched the reaction against this under Richards and although he approved the new criticism of Richards, Leavis and Empson he showed no real sympathy with textual studies. Greg and Pollard each had one brief mention while McKerrow had none at all. The precise situation at Cambridge was one upon which he commented:

'Further it would be wrong to make too much of the controversy Eliot aroused, as if there were no other subjects on which the opinions of the English staff were divided. One of these was textual criticism and bibliography. How seriously should you take them? There was a minority who took them very seriously indeed. I remember discussing with Attwater what annotated edition of Shakespeare the undergraduates had better use for their set plays. He favoured the Arden because the textual notes came not at the end but in great prominence immediately under the text; and to establish his point he limped across the room to fetch one of the red quartos of this edition. I have not forgotten the unchallengeable earnestness of his expression as he pointed to a thick little nest of variant readings and conjectures below the text and said, "There, that's what I mean." To work myself up into any comparable state

[1] *TILLYARD*, E. M. W. *The Muse Unchained: an intimate account of the revolution in English studies at Cambridge*, 1958.

of earnestness was beyond me; all too plainly I lacked the necessary emotional equipment to pass a comment on his remark. But I no more dared question his reverence in front of the textual variants than if he had taken me for a silent walk through a cemetery, suddenly stopped, and then pointing to a monument, remarked, "There, that's my mother's grave." '

'So, in some queer sort of way textual criticism tugged at Attwater's heart and he was anxious that in doing the set plays of Shakespeare the undergraduates should know the chief textual problems they contained; but he never formed a party of textual critics, he never hinted that all the best people thought textual criticism an absolute'.

When dealing in the same book with the arrival of H. S. Bennett on the faculty Tillyard wrote, 'With his bent to bibliography and social history he has never been in full sympathy with what for good or ill has been the distinguishing achievement of the Cambridge English School.' He also stated that 'Attwater and Bennett inclined to the Oxford habit of promoting editions of texts.'

That so easy a dismissal of bibliography as a tool of any importance in the study of literature could be made in 1958 by so established a practitioner is a clear indication that bibliography has not yet proved its case. In Oxford, as Tillyard had suggested, the textual tradition was stronger. The new bibliography can be regarded as having had official recognition there as far back as 1913 when Percy Simpson conducted his first classes in bibliographical method and the applications of textual criticism. Yet even Oxford can produce sceptics. At the Fourth Conference of the International Association of University Professors of English held in August 1959, F. W. Bateson read a paper on 'Modern bibliography and the literary artifact'.[1]

Bateson admitted that he was only using the Higher Bibliography as a stalking horse for the bigger game of the Formalist

---

[1] *English Studies Today*: Second Series. Francke Verlag. Bern. 1961. pp. 67–77.

Fallacy in literary criticism, As a starting point he took two statements of Fredson Bowers. One was a paragraph from Bowers' *On Editing Shakespeare and the Elizabethan Dramatists.* 'When bibliography and textual criticism join (sc. in the editing of a definitive text), it is impossible to imagine one without the other. Bibliography may be said to attack textual problems from the mechanical point of view, using evidence which must deliberately avoid being coloured by literary considerations. Non-bibliographical textual criticism works with meanings and literary values. If these last are divorced from all connection with the evidence of the mechanical process that imprinted meaningful symbols on a sheet of paper, no check-rein of fact or probability can restrain the farthest reaches of idle speculation.'[1] Second, Bateson said that he wished to take up the challenge of Fredson Bowers made at a meeting of the English Institute some years previously that he could prove 'on physical evidence not subject to opinion' that Shakespeare wrote *sallied flesh* and not *solid flesh* in *Hamlet* (1, ii, 129).

Bateson's point was that, since Bowers had chosen the ground on which to fight, the whole issue could be decided on this particular case. 'If the claim fails here, on bibliography's home ground as it were, it is perhaps not likely to be made good elsewhere.' Bateson argued that *sallied* (the reading in both the bad Q1 and the good Q2) and the Folio reading of *solid* are near enough alike to argue a common origin and not the revision of an earlier reading. Bateson rejected any conclusion of Bowers' as being 'proof' of the correctness of *sullied* as the true reading here for the text and therefore argued himself into the position in which he claimed that only non-bibliographical considerations could determine the true meaning. 'These historical certainties have not been married, however, to the linguistic problem "Which word is Shakespeare most likely to have used?", still less to its aesthetic extension "Which was the *right* word for Shakespeare to have used?" Bateson's argument was, therefore

[1] *BOWERS*, Fredson. *On Editing Shakespeare and the Elizabethan Dramatists.* University of Pennsylvania. 1955.

developed on the familiar lines of the necessity for an adjective which denotes the state of flesh as 'supremely rigid, *frozen stiff*', and he concluded that ' "Solid flesh" is better English, better Shakespeare, better poetry'; three judgements which are highly personal ones and equally not susceptible of 'proof'.

Alice Walker, formerly Reader in Textual Bibliography at Oxford, and greeted by Bateson as 'the shrewdest of the bibliotextualists', gave considerable support to his views.[1] Reviewing his paper, Dr Walker argued, 'What is strictly bibliographical in Mr Bowers's case against the "solid flesh" is no more than that Q1 and Q2 agree in reading "sallied" (an agreement which may only signify that Q2 reproduced an error of Q1) and that a different Q2 compositor set up "sallies" (=sullies) at ii.1.39. It is not, however, a bibliographical fact that two compositors would not make the same error. This is the inference of a bibliographer . . . The position is that the critic of *Hamlet* is at liberty to choose in this case the reading which is, in sense and style, the more appropriate to the context.'

The consensus of opinion here, and it would be echoed by many other literary scholars, is, in Bateson's words, 'that bibliographical evidence – in the strict sense of the term – does not *mesh* as it were, with stylistic evidence'. If, however, this is true, then the reverse of the proposition can be said to be of equal validity. Literary evidence cannot be accepted uncritically if it does not *mesh* with the supporting bibliographical evidence. A fact which is occasionally overlooked in the flurry of argument is that the ultimate source of all the evidence, the text which the author intended to write, is constant. All kinds of evidence must, consequently, point in the same direction if it is good, reliable, evidence. It is only our traditional habits and our inbred suspicion of new developments which cause us to prefer one variety of evidence over another. It should be possible to see, in all the areas of evidence, an attempt to reconcile their inconsistencies and to establish a firm basis of

---

[1] *The Library*: Fifth series: Vol. XVII (1962) pp. 271–72.

textual material for critical study. Out of textual work of the past it is, however, all too easy to find examples of work in which no attempt was made to give due weight respectively to literary and bibliographical evidence. In such examples it appears inevitable that it is the literary evidence which is advanced to the detriment, and indeed the exclusion, of any considerations of a bibliographical nature even at the most unsophisticated level. Nowhere is this conflict more clearly illustrated than in the monstrous perversions which Bentley proposed for the text of Milton. Bateson can urge that 'Bibliography battens on man's superstitious reverence for the written word', but literary critics can sometimes be accused of having ignored the marks made on the pieces of paper when they ran counter to their own particular theories. One could only wish that Bentley had shown a little more superstitious reverence for the written word when on purely literary grounds he emended,

> *They hand in hand with wand'ring Steps and slow*
> *Through Eden took their solitary way*

to read

> *Then hand in hand with Social steps their way*
> *Through Eden took, with Heav'nly Comfort cheer'd*

or when in place of

> *Ye that in Waters glide, and ye that walk*
> *The Earth, and stately tread, or lowly creep*

Bentley suggested the reading,

> *Beasts, that these Groves frequent, both ye that walk*
> *With stately tread, and ye that lowly creep.*

Unhappily, Bentley was applying the test which Bateson required, 'Which was the *right* word for Milton to have used?' Bentley could surely, as did Bateson, defend his reading as 'better English, better Milton, better poetry'. Emendations made without recourse to the written word are dangerous in the extreme.

When Fredson Bowers delivered his Sandars lectures in 1958 he gave instances of literary critics of some eminence who could be found discussing the importance of a reading which, on bibliographical grounds, could be shown to be corrupt.[1] Two examples may be given of the lack of critical interest in a correct text such as Bowers instanced in his first lecture.

'Criticism of modern literature as if it were written by seventeenth-century "metaphysicals" has produced various admirable treatises, but sometimes the approval of *discordia concors* is carried to the lengths of extravagant praise for the *discordia* of a printer's error without the *concors* of the poet's intention. Such an instance is found in F. O. Matthiesen's discussion of a phrase of Herman Melville's in *White-Jacket*. Melville is describing his fall into the sea from the yard-arm of the U.S. frigate *Neversink*. In the Constable Standard Edition of Melville's *Works* we read the following description of his feelings as he floats under water in an almost trance-like state:

"I wondered whether I was yet dead or still dying. But of a sudden some fashionless form brushed my side – some inert, soiled fish of the sea; the thrill of being alive again tingled in my nerves, and the strong shunning of death shocked me through."

'Commenting on these lines Matthieson writes:

"But then this second trance is shattered by a twist of imagery of the sort that was to become peculiarly Melville's. He is startled back into the sense of being alive by grazing an inert form; hardly anyone but Melville could have created the shudder that results from calling this frightening vagueness some 'soiled fish of the sea'. The *discordia concors*, the unexpected linking of the medium of cleanliness with filth, could only have sprung from an imagination that had apprehended the terrors of the deep, of the immaterial deep as well as the physical."

'The only difficulty with this critical *frisson* about Melville's imagination, and undemonstrable generalizations such as "nobody but Melville could have created the shudder", and so

---

[1] *BOWERS*, Fredson. *Textual and Literary Criticism.* 1959.

on, is the cruel fact that an unimaginative type-setter inadvertently created it, not Melville; for what Melville wrote, as is demonstrated in both the English and American first editions, was *coiled* fish of the sea. It is disheartening to find the enthusiasm of critics so easily betrayed; . . .'[1]

This instance was followed by another.

'In the matter of finding preferential literary excellences in misprints Professor Empson is a frequent offender by reason of his careless use of imperfect texts, complicated by a more than ordinary inaccuracy of quotation from these texts. I can only mention in passing his gaffe in *Seven Types of Ambiguity* in which he argues most persuasively for an added eeriness in Eliot's 'Whispers of Immortality' caused by the slight doubt about the syntax in the tenth, eleventh and twelfth lines (a doubt materially aided by his punctuating of the twelfth line in a way not found in any Eliot text). In fact, on the ambiguity of the syntax he ultimately comes to the position that "This I take to be the point of the poem and it is conveyed by the contradictory ways of taking the grammar."

'Well, when a critic arrives at conclusions about the point of a poem that are reached through the interpretations of printer's errors in the text, we may see how readily white may be made black, and black white, and we may be forgiven if we treat his opinions in general with some reserve. The truth is that Empson studied Eliot, and spun his finely drawn theories about Eliot's literary art, not from the relatively pure first or second editions, but from either the third or fourth edition. By bad luck a printer's common transpositional error in the third edition exchanged the terminal punctuation of lines 10 and 11, making the end of the sentence come at line 10 instead of line 11, and wrongly beginning a new sentence with the final infinitive phrase of the correct old sentence; and the mistake was not caught up until the sixth edition. On the evidence of the periodical text of the poem, followed by its first two book editions, and

[1] *ibid.* pp. 29–30.

145

the correction of the sixth edition, it was the faulty printer – and not the poet – who introduced the syntactical ambiguity that Empson so greatly admired and felt was the point of the whole poem.'[1]

Examples such as these can be multiplied to show that a matter of some importance is raised when a choice is made of an edition of a literary work for study. It is not only the factual and interpretative notes which may vary, as Attwater tried to point out to Tillyard, but the text itself and frequently in matters of some importance. It has been a distinctive contribution of modern American bibliography to force upon us the realization that this problem concerns current productions equally with those of earlier periods.

In the 'perpetuated misprint' correspondence in the *Times Literary Supplement* in 1959, M. R. Ridley raised a similar problem chiefly in the works of R. L. Stevenson.[2] Early printing errors which had escaped notice were carried forward in edition after edition with little or no attempt by the critics to elucidate the text sufficiently. Small and relatively unimportant as some of these changes seemed to be, others were of considerable importance; but in either case the text could not be said to be established until bibliographical considerations had been taken into account. Once again, a voice was raised welcoming the application of bibliographical reasoning to modern books. John Sparrow wrote, 'I am glad that Mr Ridley should have reinforced, with some striking examples of errors in modern texts of Stevenson and others, the case so often and so authoritatively urged by Dr R. W. Chapman, in your columns and elsewhere, against the common delusion that textual criticism has no place in dealing with modern, printed texts.'[3]

Other instances have occurred in which investigations have led to re-appraisals of authorship rather than of the establishment of the text. One of the most noteworthy in this field was

---

[1] *ibid*. pp. 31–32.
[2] *Times Literary Supplement*. 28 August 1959.
[3] *Times Literary Supplement*. 11 September 1959.

announced in John Crow's article 'Marlowe yields to Jervis Markham'.[1] When Robert Allott published *England's Parnassus* in 1600, he placed the names of authors at the end of the extracts from their works. Among these was one twenty-four line extract beginning, 'I walked along a stream for pureness rare', and attributed by Allott to 'Ch. Marlow'.[2] This extract consisted of two complete stanzas, preceded by one half stanza and followed by another. Over the years literary critics have not simply accepted this ascription to Marlowe, they have found in them a true example of Marlowe's genius. Tucker Brooke wrote, 'The lines must be accepted as work of the poet's full maturity, parallel in date as in tone with "Hero and Leander". They are a valuable evidence of Marlowe's versatility for they indicate the possession of an aptitude for graceful stanzaic verse after the Spenserian fashion which no other extant production of his attests.'[3]

John Bakeless wrote, 'Whatever the story of their origin may be, the lines in *England's Parnassus* have the genuine Marlowe ring, and there is no reason for questioning their authenticity – especially as five of the twenty-four lines are run on, much in Marlowe's manner, which was by no means common at this period.'[4]

F. S. Boas wrote, 'Short as it is, this specimen serves to show that Marlowe could handle the elaborate rhyme of the poem with easy mastery. And it is marked by his characteristic boldness of imagery and wealth of colour . . . The comparison with the sun's palace gate is in the true Marlovian vein as, in different wise, is the similitude in the next stanza of the trees overarching the stream to "a costly valance o'er a bed".'[5]

Crow was, however, able to identify the original work from which Allott took his extract. It was 'DEVOREVX. Vertues

---

[1] *Times Literary Supplement.* 4 January 1947.

[2] Number 2240 in Oxford edition of *England's Parnassus*. 1913.

[3] *P.M.L.A.A.* 1922.

[4] *BAKELESS*, John. *The Tragicall History of Christopher Marlowe.* 1942. Vol. 2 p. 160.

[5] *BOAS*, F. S. *Christopher Marlowe.* 1940. p. 222.

teares for the losse of the most Christian King *Henry*, third of that name, King of *Fraunce*; and the vntimely death, of the most noble & heroicall Gentleman, *VValter Deuoreux*, who was slain before *Roan* in Fraunce. First written in French, by the most excellent and learned Gentlewoman, Madam *Genenuefue*, *Petau Maulette*. And paraphrastically translated into English, *Jeruis Markham* . . . 1597!'[1] Only two copies of this book are recorded, one in the Henry Huntington Library in California and the other in the Bodleian. Knowing that Crawford, the best editor of *England's Parnassus* to date, used Malone's copy for his text, or more probably a photo-copy of it. Crow was able to list a number of important variants and so make a beginning on the establishment of the text.

In these examples, different kinds of bibliographical investigation have been used in order to counterbalance the results of purely literary investigation. As Dr Boas wrote, following John Crow's first article on Jervase Markham, 'This will surely become a classic example, that we must take to heart, of the dangers that beset conclusions drawn from internal evidence.'[2]

In spite of an increasing number of examples of this nature a certain amount of expert, and not entirely hostile, criticism has been directed at the claims of modern bibliography. In notable recent instances they have come from Dr Alice Walker, herself a bibliographer and pupil of Greg.

When she reviewed Bower's *Textual and Literary Criticism* she wrote, 'It would be foolish to suppose that bibliography will displace the older (and maturer) disciplines of linguistic and literary criticism. What we need to be sure about is where one way of tackling problems ends and another begins.'[3] This has been a problem ever since bibliography began and was a major difference between the attitudes of McKerrow and Greg. They had always understood this difference themselves. In his *Prolegomena*, McKerrow had written, 'It is, I think, very unfortun-

[1] S.T.C. 19793.
[2] *Times Literary Supplement.* 18 January 1947.
[3] *Review of English Studies.* New Series. Vol. XI (1960) pp. 449–451.

ate that attempts to determine the causes of the condition of the texts seem to have come to be called by the general name of "bibliographical" study of these texts. The only reason for the name seems to be that some of the principal scholars who have interested themselves in such research, such as Dr A. W. Pollard and Dr W. W. Greg, have *also* been bibliographers. There is nothing particularly 'bibliographical' about most of the arguments used.'[1] Equally, Greg in his memoir of McKerrow wrote of the studies described as, 'What I should have annoyed him by calling the bibliographical criticism of dramatic texts.'[2]

There is a very obvious need for a clarification of terminology here, yet the main outlines of the disagreement between McKerrow and Greg can be seen. Recently, Dr Walker has appeared to support the McKerrow line. In a review of S. K. Sen's *Capell and Malone and Modern Critical Bibliography* she took the 'opportunity of protesting against the use of the term "critical bibliography".[3] It is, I suppose, generally agreed that the bibliographer is best qualified to construct a stemma for printed books; but, unless the recension provides an editor with a fool-proof text, it is the business of the textual critic to discriminate between true and false readings. Let us therefore use the traditional term "textual criticism", so that everyone knows what we are talking about, instead of "critical bibliography", which confounds what is strictly bibliographical (in the sense in which McKerrow used the word) and what is strictly the business of experts in other fields.'[4]

Again, in her review of Bateson's paper, Dr Walker wrote, 'The chief mischief comes of allowing far too much to pass as "bibliographical". If the term were restricted to the sense in

[1] *McKERROW*, R. B. *Prolegomena to the Oxford Shakespeare.* 1939. p. 9.

[2] *GREG*, W. W. Memoir of McKerrow in *The Proceedings of the British Academy.* Vol. XXVI.

[3] *SEN*, S. K. *Capell and Malone, and modern critical bibliography.* Calcutta. Mukhopadhyay. 1960.

[4] *The Library*: Fifth Series: Vol XVI (1961). pp. 310–311.

which McKerrow used it, there would be less pother between bibliographers and literary critics."[1] It is impossible to escape the conclusion, however, that in many instances of criticism which have appeared in recent years along these lines, it is not Greg's view of bibliography which is being attacked but rather that the real target is the same as that identified by name by Bateson in his lecture: Fredson Bowers.

Fredson Bowers first began to claim general attention on the publication of his *Principles of Bibliographical Description* in 1949.[2] The first of the important qualifications which he made in this work was that 'this present book endeavors to follow such a concept by which bibliography is largely taken in its primary meaning as *analytical bibliography* . . . In general, when bibliographical evidence is discussed, the point of view is that of *analytical bibliography*.' Bowers was to say almost the same thing when he came to write the article on 'Bibliography' in the *Encyclopaedia Britannica*. In all the many discussions which Bowers has conducted the distinguishing basic feature of bibliography is that it concerns itself with the discovery and recording of the physical facts about the book. This would never, at any stage of bibliographical history, have been doubted. Bowers, however, has continued his argument to the effect that the assembly of these facts was not primarily to aid the book collector or the librarian to identify his copies. This was a legitimate side-product of bibliography but the main importance of all the work was 'as the penultimate step to textual and literary criticism'.

It is mainly in his work in descriptive bibliography and textual bibliography that Bowers has made his major contribution and, at the same time, aroused the chief opposition.

In descriptive bibliography Bowers has been regarded as being too much of a perfectionist. 'The concern of the descriptive bibliographer. . . is to examine every available copy of an

---

[1] *The Library*: Fifth Series: Vol XVII (1962) p. 272.
[2] BOWERS, Fredson. *Principles of Bibliographical Description*. 1949 . (Re-issue 1962)

edition of a book in order to describe in bibliographical terms the characteristics of an ideal copy of this edition, to distinguish between issues and variants of the edition, to explain and describe the printing and textual history of the edition, and finally to arrange it in a correct and logical relationship to other editions.' He has stressed insistently the necessity to examine all available copies and this procedure, considered unnecessary in the days of bibliographical innocence and the belief in the unity of the edition, has gradually won wider acceptance as the individual status of the copy has been increasingly realized. He has demanded a description which is exhaustive, which sets out to solve the bibliographical problems of the work, and which employs a clear and precise terminology. For bibliographical compilations which do not reach these standards Bowers proposed separate terminology; Catalogue, Descriptive Catalogue, Bibliographical Catalogue.

The same kind of precision and exacting standards have been apparent in Bowers' other work and one major area of disagreement has revolved around his claims for textual bibliography as a legitimate and important part of textual criticism. In his Sandars Lectures he discussed the importance of bibliography in providing evidence of a factual nature which leads to an emendation of the text. In the light of the experience of this century it would be foolish to deny the nature of the application of such bibliographical evidence. What is more debatable is the relative importance of this kind of evidence and its relationship to more established forms of evidence in textual criticism. To some critics it is a matter of concern that Bowers has not seen fit to work in scholarly solitude but, more so than any other bibliographer, has gone some way towards the foundation of a school. The Bibliographical Society of the University of Virginia, in which Bowers was Professor of English Literature, was founded soon after the end of World War II. It began the publication of its Papers, later entitled 'Studies in Bibliography', in 1948 and it is in this series that much of the main work of 'the Bowers School' has appeared. One of the earliest papers of general interest to textual studies, printed here was R. C. Bald's 'Editorial problems – a preliminary survey'.[1] Bald demonstrated that the major editorial problem was that of the establishment of the text but that, occasionally, this was a duty of the editor which was not accepted in any measure. 'Within the past year or so two new college *Shakespeares* have appeared, [G. B. Harrison, *Shakespeare, Twenty-Three Plays and Sonnets*; O. J. Campbell, *The Living Shakespeare*] whose editors are perhaps the two most active and distinguished Shakespearian scholars in the country. For range and interest of material presented in introductions and notes, the two books are a marked improvement on anything previously available, and they are bound to exert a strong influence on the teaching of Shakespeare for a generation or so. Yet both reproduce the Globe text. It is not as if there had been no advances in the textual study of Shakespeare during the present century, nor are these two editors ignorant of the work of Pollard, McKerrow, Greg and Dover Wilson; but is there any other branch of study in which a teacher would be satisfied to present students, as these books do, with the results achieved by scholarship up to, but not beyond, the year 1864?'[2]

It is this insistence that modern bibliographical work has something quite distinct and of value to offer to the literary critic which has rung so loudly in the writings in *Studies in Bibliography*. As bibliographical expertise has increased throughout the years so attempts have been made to demonstrate how editorial practices might be affected by the new material. It has been applied to texts of all periods. Not unnaturally, Shakespeare has received the bulk of attention.

The final justification for much of this detailed working and the rebuttal of those who fear that bibliography, under the aegis of Bowers, is turning itself into an end unto itself surely lies in the bibliographically based editions which have emerged as a result of these activities. Fredson Bowers' editions of

[1] *Studies in Bibliography*. Vol. III. (1950–51). pp. 3–17.
[2] *ibid.* p. 5.

Dekker[1]; of Whitman's *Leaves of Grass*[2]; and of Hawthorne's *Scarlet letter*[3] all reach levels of textual exactitude not achieved in anything which had preceded them for those authors.

All the evidence produced seems to suggest that, at this particular moment of bibliographical studies, a measure of disagreement exists as to the validity of some of the work now being done. On the one hand there are bibliographers who believe implicitly in the importance of the study in its applications to textual studies although their claims are, perhaps, rarely as dogmatic as certain of their critics are anxious to suggest. On the far extreme there is a comparatively small body of literary critics who appear to deny the role of bibliography as having any importance at all in this respect.

In the words of F. W. Bateson in the summing up of his arguments at the end of his Conference paper: 'Analytical bibliography is a discipline in its own right, but its findings are likely to be of only marginal interest to the student of literature, (a) because its concern is not with literary meanings but with the process by which the printing press distributes written words, and (b) because the written word itself is only a spatial translation of the oral and temporal original.'

It is necessary, therefore, to summarize the chief accomplishments of bibliography after approximately a century of bibliographical research in the modern manner and approximately half of a century of effort in trying to apply the evidence of bibliography to the problems of the text.

One fact has been made abundantly clear. In the study of a particular work or text it is imperative to isolate that part of the problem which may be capable of bibliographical analysis. Clarification of this issue would go a long way towards meeting the legitimate concern of those who fear lest bibliography

[1] *BOWERS*, Fredson. *ed. The Dramatic Works of Thomas Dekker*, 4 vols. 1953–1961.

[2] *BOWERS*, Fredson. *ed. Whitman's Manuscripts: Leaves of Grass* (1860). A parallel text. University of Chicago Press. 1955.

[3] *BOWERS*, Fredson. *Textual editor. Nathaniel Hawthorne: centenary edition.* Ohio State University Press. 1963 – in progress.

should try to involve itself, and make pronouncements upon, problems which are not bibliographical. At first glance the direct contribution which can be made to the study of a particular book or text by this means may appear to be slight, but not infrequently it may be crucial.

W. A. Jackson gave two examples of this kind of isolation when addressing students on the relationship between bibliography and literary studies.[1] 'As an example of this I have often cited a not too recent book by an eminent historian, a colleague and friend of mine, on the Marian exiles. In this book there is a long chapter regarding Bishop Aylmer's *An harborowe for faithfull subiectes*, 1559, which says on the title that it was printed in "Strasborowe". After what undoubtedly was a laborious search of the registers of aliens in various cities of Europe, my friend traces the wanderings of Bishop Aylmer in 1559 and records that he was apparently in several cities of Germany in that year, but not in Strassburg. His final conclusion is that the book might have been printed in any one of the various cities which the author had visited, but that it probably was not printed in Strassburg.

'Now, a glance at the book would have shown that is has distinctive types, ornaments and initials that to someone familiar with such things would probably be identifiable. There are many people who would be able to say off-hand that the book was English printed and certainly there are several who, with very little effort indeed, could positively identify the ornaments and initials and testify that the book was printed in London by John Day. This was a bibliographical problem which, if approached in a bibliographical way, would have been solved with certainty and dispatch.

'Sometimes the difficulty has been not in the failure to look, but in looking at the wrong thing, a corrupt edition of a facsimile which is inadequate. The classic example of this last was pointed out by the late R. W. Chambers in his edition of A. J.

[1] *JACKSON*, W. A. *Bibliography and Literary Studies*. University of California. 1962.

Wyatt's *Beowulf*. You have doubtless all seen the charred and crinkled Cottonian manuscript of that prime work of Anglo-Saxon literature in the British Museum. Most scholars, however, have perforce had to use Zupitza's facsimile of it, which although it an excellent one is, as Chambers observes, no substitute for an examination of the manuscript itself, for that manuscript has to be turned in many ways, and examined under many lights before the stroke of a letter can be distinguished from some accidental crease.

'An American scholar thought he saw in the facsimile an erased word, *heado*, in an admittedly defective passage (62–3). Later when Chambers examined the original manuscript and held it up to the light, the dim marks, which in the facsimile (and at first sight in the manuscript also) look like fragments of an erased word, turned out to be nothing more than strokes of a word on the other side of the leaf, which, as so often in the *Beowulf* manuscript, show through the parchment. The discussion of the "erased word" and the theories built upon it was the subject of seven contributions to a philological journal consisting of about ten thousand printed words. Chambers, disregarding the misspent labour of the scholars, remarked only, "It is painful to think that the time of skilled compositors should have thus been wasted." '

In each of these instances the actual bibliographical contribution is a relatively small one but, again, in each case the implications of that fact upon, in the one case, the history of the text and, in the other case, the actual interpretation of the text are considerable. The former serves as a reminder of Lawrence Wroth's warning that bibliographical evidence has frequently been undervalued in historical investigations[1] and the latter as a reminder that the danger of such facsimiles is still with us.

No one would attempt to make bibliography play a larger part in textual problems than the very nature of the evidence

---

[1] *WROTH*, L. C. 'The bibliographical way', *The Colophon*. New series. Vol III (1938) pp. 225–237.

makes practicable. No one would attempt to justify a claim that bibliography comprises the whole of textual criticism. The recognition which bibliographers now seek should be that textual criticism rests on a firm basis of historical, literary, philological, and bibliographical evidence. The first three have long been accepted as valid evidence, the fourth can now be regarded as of equal repute even if not invariably of equal importance.

The most important single contribution which bibliography has made so far relates to the individuality of the copy. This is a state of affairs which has largely been brought about by the development and increased usage of modern bibliographical methods. In the paper which he read to the Bibliographical Society on 18th December, 1911, on 'The Duplicity of Duplicates' Falconer Madan drew attention to the variants which could normally be expected in studying books printed prior to 1800. Even so, his concern was primarily that of the librarian who had to exercise due care and caution in discarding. There was no suggestion at this time that the multiplication of copies might indeed have some positive value. 'I do *not*,' he wrote, 'advocate the collection of duplicates (that way madness lies) . . . .' He could only imagine the ownership of two copies of the First Folio in the event of being a Pierpont Morgan. The amassing of seventy-nine copies of the book as at the Folgar Library would probably have puzzled him as it has puzzled many people since his time. Increasingly, however, as modern methods of collating books have been perfected, an awareness has grown of the variants, trivial and important, between copies of an edition which ought, by all the laws of evidence, to be identical. This has culminated in Hinman's study.

The results of this awareness have been two-fold. Care must be taken in the selection of any individual copy of a pre-1800 book for the purposes of literary comment or discussion. A statement, previously acceptable, that, for example, 'the text is that of the 1598 edition' is now barely adequate for scholarly purposes. Because of the measure of disagreement between copies, increasing care has been taken over the exact specification of detail, especially in collation, in descriptive bibliography. Greg's original survey of this problem was elaborated by Bowers in his *Principles of Bibliographical Description* and Greg produced his final and fullest statement in the fourth volume of his *Bibliography of English Printed Drama to the Restoration*. Although Greg's viewpoint differed in detail from that of Bowers, with whom he admitted he did not always see 'eye to eye', his detail in the collational formula is no less exacting to the initial inquirer. This has probably in some measure led critics to suggest that description at this level defeats its main objective in conveying essential information to literary students who are confused rather than helped by the system. It is also the fear of some bibliographers that, at this level of complexity, bibliography may increasingly be pursued as a study for its own sake and without due concern for the use which it can be to literary studies as a whole. In fact, one charge now levelled against bibliography in general is that it concerns itself overmuch with the mass of detail which the improvements of its methods now makes available to it. This allegation is heard as frequently with reference to its impact upon textual studies as upon descriptive work. F. W. Bateson, in the paper already referred to, complained that 'to insist on the editor inflicting his author's "accidentals" of spelling, capitalization and punctuation on the modern reader, as Greg and McKerrow do, is to confuse the the function of an author with that of his copyist. It is true most authors are their own copyists, but the talents and training required in the two functions are quite distinct.' Dr Alice Walker in her review of Bateson's paper supported his argument. She contended that now that it was known how much the accidentals of a printed book depended upon the vagaries of compositors or printing houses they should be regarded as 'merely a part of the evidence for the recension of a text'. In a critically edited text she concluded that what was 'accidental and adventitious to the sense should not be allowed to intervene between author and reader' and that when more is required a photographic reproduction of the original is necessary.[1]

Objections such as these show a concern that bibliographical method is currently capable of producing detail in greater quantity than some critics appear to regard as useful. The oddity of this contention lies in the fact that it ignores the range of edited texts of a work which are required: from those which, designed for scholarly purposes, must take note of the most recent and detailed work of every kind which has been done on the text, to those which, designed for popular usage, should nevertheless be based on a scholarly edition. No one would seriously contend that the general reader should have the author's 'accidentals' paraded before him in his text, but no one should deny that these have a value to the specialist scholar.

Equally it should by now be commonly accepted that the most popular edition of a text should accept the readings which have been established by the scholarly editions. It is cynical in the extreme to assume that any text, however discredited, however old and surpassed by modern scholarship, will serve the purposes of the general reader. Greg demonstrated the practicability and the value of this appreciation of the variety needed when he published his two editions of *Doctor Faustus*. One was a parallel text edition of the two texts of 1604 and 1616 with a full apparatus of critical notes and an introduction and notes which together were double the length of the text itself. It is right that a text conceived on these lines should be available. On the same day of publication of this edition Greg also issued a small, slim volume containing 'a conjectural reconstruction' of the same play suited to the needs of the general reader. Variations in the purpose of editions of this nature are an important part of editorial function and all levels of bibliographical emphasis can be recorded. It is, consequently, difficult to generalize and to suggest that bibliographical minutiae are always irrelevant,

The purpose of bibliography applied to textual studies is

---

[1] *The Library*: Fifth Series: Vol XVII (1962) p. 272.

to enable the text to be established as near as is practicable to that which the author intended. Any variation from that desired text of the author must, in general, be something which has resulted from the physical nature of the book, the understanding of which is the main role of bibliography. Therefore, the attempt is made to peel away the layers of intervening printing and publishing house accretion in order to reveal the author's true text. Priority must be given to the evidence which can be accounted for by the known practices of the time and not by changing standards of literary values. This attempt to produce a text 'according unto his owen makying', as Caxton wrote of his edition of Chaucer, is no new feature. What is novel is the increasing emphasis which is being given to this kind of editing and the development of the tools which are making the analysis possible.

In its short life bibliography has already made some contributions to textual studies. Due to its researches we now know much more of the sequence of printings of the Shakespearian quartos and folios and the relationship between them. We understand more of the complexities of Blake's editions, of nineteenth-century novels and of early printings of the *Lyrical Ballads*. If we are no longer presented with editions with readings such as 'soldier Aristotle' or 'soiled fish' this is directly attributable to bibliography. The advances may seem small but, equally, we now have editions of Nashe or Dekker which are more reputable than their predecessors even if they cannot be regarded as final definitive editions. A connection has been shown to exist between the processes of writing and printing, of book manufacture and the text which is carried on the pages. That may not be an insignificant contribution to have made so early on in the lifetime of a newly emerging study.

7
Historical bibliography

The area regarding which there has been least argument in the definition of bibliography is that of 'historical bibliography'. This has generally been seen to be a neatly circumscribed area devoted to the history of the book and there, broadly speaking, the matter has rested. This was logical for so long as a definition of history itself could be dismissed summarily as 'things which have happened'. By analogy with this historical bibliography was simply what has happened within the fields of bibliographical interest and the manufacture of books.

This should not be regarded as specifically incorrect, yet it has in the past imposed uncharacteristic limitations on the subject. The tendency has been for the history of the book to be primarily the account of its production and, to a lesser extent, its dissemination, but without any particular purpose being discussed for its existence. The book itself as a term for the subject of the study must be treated in a very wide context. It is not the 'book' in the modern sense which is the concern of historical bibliography, but rather, Greg's own words, 'every sort of record made by the symbolic representation of language'. The waxed tablets, papyrus rolls and codices, baked clay tablets, even wall paintings provided they were attempts to communicate are all the subjects of study. The purpose of the material provides the main criterion for the inclusion of certain items. I. R. Willison defined it as 'the physical characteristics of printed books considered in their historical aspect, or, more precisely and academically, mass-produced texts as technical, commercial and cultural-political artefacts which have realized and (so to speak) substantiated in history the *intention* of authors and publishers to control opinion, to advance learning, to make money or to express sensibility. Historical bibliography, in short, is the study of books as *direct* evidence of almost all those various movements towards literacy and self-determination which have constituted the general history of Europe since the renaissance.'[1]

As the cultural environment of mankind advanced man's desire to communicate with his fellows demanded something more permanent, more expressive than speech. Certain of his media of communication, therefore, left behind them some kind of deliberate, permanent, or would-be-so record. In general, records which were not designed by their originators to possess a degree of permanency should normally be regarded as outside the field of historical bibliography. From clay tablets onwards we have an unending series of differing physical media which attempted to perform this preserving function. It is thus an easy step to understand why Greg should be prepared to consider even the eventual inclusion of 'phonograph records'.

The passage of time must, inevitably, add other material forms to those already in use for the permanent recording of ideas and these will equally become a part of the whole bibliographical world. It is at the moment of such realization that we recall the variety of the media of the past and the fact that the printed book, so often the sole repository of bibliographical research, is a comparatively new and short-lived phenomenon. Historical bibliography should reveal the whole chain of physical forms which have served their term while the main function of the 'book' has continued relatively undisturbed.

Because these 'books' are not end-products in themselves but simply pieces of equipment to enable the essential function to

---

[1] *SEWELL*, P. H. *ed. Five Years' Work in Librarianship, 1951–1955.* 1958. p. 330.

be performed it is an increasingly sterile occupation to regard their history in too narrow a sense.

The history of the book is a part of the social and cultural life of the people of its time; the history of its production and distribution is a part of technological and economic history. Some of the aspects of its decorative elements are a part of the history of art. Quite late on in his career, Greg was prepared to dismiss the claims of decorative binding styles as belonging to decorative leather work in general without, normally, any connection with bibliography.

In the introduction to his *Copy and Print in the Netherlands* W. G. Hellinga wrote, 'The task of cultural history comprises, according to the classic definition of the grand-master of that history, Huizinga, the amassing of information about the nature and progress of the phenomena of civilization in general. To the subjects with which this study ought to concern itself belong the history of universal themes such as sentiments and symbols, that of religious and ethnological phenomena, such as games and sacred rites, and finally the history of entities that are not of a purely spiritual nature but also have a material form, such as fashions, the house, the garden, the inn, etc. Books belong to this last group. . . Whoever sets out to write the cultural history of the book, therefore, will have to bear in mind three aspects of the question: the significance of books in a culture, the place of the book trade in the social order, and the outward appearance of the book in relation to other, related cultural forms.'[1]

This view must lie at the heart of any modern attempt to explain the role of historical bibliography and its relationship to the whole corpus of bibliographical knowledge. Here, as in other areas, we are acutely aware of a change in the traditional attitudes. The earliest of any of the attempts to write the history of the book were essentially limited to that aspect which Hellinga termed 'the outward appearance of the book'. Gaze

[1] *HELLINGA*, Wytze Gs. *Copy and Print in the Netherlands. An atlas of historical bibliography*. North-Holland Publishing Company. 1962.

was turned inward upon the book and its supporting trade without very much relationship to the cultural life of the community of which it formed a part. As potent a reason as any for this fact that much of the historical writing had been a thinly disguised emotional antiquarianism. Writers such as Dibdin were primarily concerned with the cult of the book collector and historical apparatus was chiefly of value because it provided a background against which the rarity of a book, and hence to some extent its value, could be assessed.

This still operates to a very real extent as can be seen by studying the annotations in the catalogues of rare book dealers. Phrases occur regularly in which the chronological element, the outstanding one in a simple interpretation of history, is to the fore. This leads eventually to the 'first edition heresy' in which the preserved earliest printing is elevated, sometimes out of all proportion, to a status far above any other printings. A first edition is always important but it is not necessarily so much more so than other, later, printings. In turn the emphasis placed on first editions becomes so exaggerated that piracies, forgeries, theft follow naturally in the wake. There are considerations other than priority which make a book of historical importance but these often have, in the past, and sometimes still are, under-appreciated.

The economic aspects of historical bibliography have, by comparison, been overshadowed. We may know that a book is of the first edition, the first book of a particular printer or from a particular town, but in the vast majority of cases we know next to nothing about its economic facts. The cost of the paper, ink and type, the rates of pay of the workmen, the relationship between the developing functions of printer, publisher and bookseller, the price at which the books were marketed – all these are largely unknown areas. Yet, with the possible exception of an extremely small minority of books, they were produced in full realization of the economic position of their time. It was a factor which influenced for good or ill every decision which was made regarding the book's manufacture and finally had its major outcome in the publication price of the book. The economic structure of the book trade is, however, still largely uninvestigated. Raw materials for research into these areas certainly exist although probably spread very unevenly over the history of book production and varying from country to country.

If the publication price of the book is frequently not known, so is also the other piece of vital information, the size of the printing in which it was made available. Upon these two factors more than any others rested eventually the range of the book's effectiveness due to the dissemination of the material. Price, size of printing, frequency of new printings, form of publication, availability of organizations, such as libraries, through which a book could be obtained – all these placed limitations upon the book's influence.

These were factors which are capable of fairly accurate measurement if sufficient research is carried out, but their final outcome lies in a direction where no quantitive assessment is possible. Books are designed with the eventual purpose of influencing the minds and actions of men and, until these results are known, the full history of the book cannot be written. It merges into the social and cultural life of its own time and succeeding generations. Only in fairly recent times has this aspect of the book trade received any considerable amount of attention. One is left with an impression that a great amount of archival material will be discovered so soon as an organized attempt is made to tackle the problems.

The technical aspects of book production from an historical viewpoint also need fuller investigation. Many problems still need to be resolved in respect of the actual methods of printing. All too few examples of the early hand press are still extant and of these only a handful are available for students to experiment upon; yet without this kind of work the solutions cannot be found. When Philip Gaskell conducted his survey in 1953 of actual models of wooden hand printing presses still extant in

Europe the sum total was nineteen.[1] No significant number has been brought to light since then and probably only a handful has been made of modern construction of the old models. Our knowledge of the actual operation of the machine which produced the whole vast mass of books between 1450 and 1800 is based primarily on written accounts. From Moxon to the early nineteenth-century printers' manuals, which still cast an interested glance at the machine which was then being gradually superseded, a generally clear picture emerges – but with significant gaps. Although early bibliographers such as Blades had begun to show evidence of real and informed interest in these problems, it was McKerrow's *Introduction* of 1927 which gave the first cohesive account in a widely available form. Some aspects of printing practice have been frequently debated since then and record can be found of discussion on topics such as the incidence of pin-holes, the dampening of sheets, etc.

The whole of McKerrow's book is aimed at giving the reader sufficient detail of printing house practice so that the operations of the press can be imaginatively studied in detail. Although McKerrow stressed the continuity of the methods involved and wrote that 'in all essentials of book production there was little difference between the methods of 1500 and those of 1800', and 'If we understand how books were produced in 1600, we shall have very little difficulty in understanding the methods of any other period', yet there are differences which are of importance. Various categories of books were dealt with very differently and this could well vary from age to age and country to country. It would be absurd to expect that a German Lutheran pamphlet of the mid-sixteenth century would be treated in the same way as an Elizabethan dramatic text in this country, or an early sixteenth-century French Book of Hours or an Italian book of romances. The analytical study of each book must be placed against the background of the methods of production and distribution appropriate to that particular category in that

---

[1] Letter in the *Times Literary Supplement*, 23 January 1953.

period. It is not only in printing and printing house techniques that this technological history is required and already seen to be required, but in all other areas also.

The history of paper manufacture and usage has been approached primarily from an economic standpoint. This is logical because it is the most important individual element among the raw materials and the one which has been most subject to outside pressures and influences. There has not so far been a comparable emphasis on the development of paper technology.

Equally we know singularly little of the development of the actual technical processes of illustration or of type founding and design. Similarly, although binding history has one of the largest bibliographies of any specialized aspect it has been almost exclusively of the decorated styles. The craft itself had hitherto been largely untouched so that, in 1963, Bernard Middleton's survey of this side of the trade broke entirely new ground.[1]

The general outline of historical bibliography is, therefore, quite clear. Some areas need reinforcement, some need a new approach but, in general, the activity as a whole can be clearly established.

While specialization has grown apace there have still been useful attempts at providing, in a single publication, a synthesis of our current knowledge of the history of the book. As the total knowledge of the field advances it becomes increasingly difficult to provide introductory volumes of this nature which reflect the current view of scholarly research and yet are capable of being appreciated by the uninitiated. *A History of the Printed Book*, which was edited by Lawrence Wroth, still takes pride of place in this particular category and the only regret is that the smallness of the edition has made it an all too uncommon work

[1] *MIDDLETON*, Bernard C. *A History of English Craft Bookbinding Technique.* 1963.

[2] *WROTH*, L. C. ed. *A History of the Printed Book*; being the third number of *The Dolphin.* 1938.

to be found by students.[2] Each generation needs to produce its own conspectus of this nature to keep pace with the advances in knowledge and to change the emphasis of the work according to current needs. What are also needed are further attempts to try to relate the whole development of the book as one of the channels of communication and to relate this growth to the general social and cultural history of the period. Professor Innes did precisely this in his *The Bias of Communication*[1]. It showed a new development in this direction and it must be the basis for further more detailed studies if our knowledge of the role of the book in man's cultural affairs is to be increased.

The next level at which profitable research might be expected to appear is concerned with the development in a particular country or area.

A source of information on historical materials which has so far been inadequately explored is that of archival and research material relating to printers and their art. The roots of historical bibliography lie in an age when the positivist approach to history in general was unknown. The great ancillary sciences such as palaeography, archaeology and such like are creations of only the last century. Although they have made significant contributions to historical studies in general, they have yet to be applied to historical bibliography in particular. When this happens a number of important results may be apparent.

Not only will the actual corpus of established fact be immeasurably greater but a number of important readjustments may occur. It is unlikely that primary source material will be more readily accessible in respect of the 'great' printers and practitioners than for the humbler members of the trades, except in one or two fortunate examples such as the Plantin archives or the Bodoni archives. Historical bibliography may, therefore, cease to be what it has tended to be in the past, a succession of studies of the great ones. The procession of outstanding printers, binders, illustrators, blinds us to the fact that, together, they were responsible for only a small percentage of

[1] *INNES*, H. A. *The Bias of Communication.* 1951.

the total output of the trade. Important as their work was in shaping the development of the book arts it was not their products which were the most widely disseminated in their own time and they were not the works which did most to create the cultural and intellectual climate of their own times.

A geographical imbalance may also be corrected. The history of printing in many countries all too readily becomes the history of printing in a limited number of major centres. Nowhere is this tendency more marked than in England. The book trade in England is largely the book trade in London. This, at least, is how it appears through the majority of general accounts. When provincial printing is covered it is sketchy in character and relatively undeveloped from one account to the next. Archives of local history material have opened up entirely new areas of historical research in recent decades and could be expected to achieve a similar result in bibliographical studies. The growing organization of Records Offices makes this an ever-present possiblity. Business archives and also some of the published accounts and histories of comparatively modest organizations are beginning to throw completely new light in formerly dark places. A high percentage of such material must be related to 'local' as opposed to national activities and it is reasonable to expect that some of the next major advances will be in these fields. Our conspectus of the national book trade and the universal development of the book can then be re-vitalized by new attitudes based on newly discovered facts.

The final area to which attention is already beginning to be paid is that of the fringe area between historical biblio-graphical studies and history and literature in general. This can take a number of forms. One of the most significant is that which is entered upon following the completion of the processes of manufacture and distribution of the book. The book is essentially a reading tool and not an end product in itself. Con-sequently, although its history in a limited sense may be complete with its distribution its purpose has yet to be fulfilled. Any survey of reading tastes and influences is, therefore, of prime concern to the bibliographer as it is to the historian or the literary critic. A number of these have been produced in recent years, most notably R. D. Alick's *The English Common Reader*.[1] Here, historical bibliography probably reaches the point at which it arrives very close to the point where textual bibliography also stands.

If the first premise in this survey is accepted, everything else will follow from it. Historical bibliography is as much a part of historical studies in general as it is of bibliographical studies. It stands in this special relationship exactly as textual bibliography does to literary studies. It can be defined in as many ways as history itself and it needs the same kind of constant resurveying and redefinition. What I have also tried to point out is that it needs just the same kind of workers in the vineyard. There is a vital part for the Namiers in the laborious and painstaking task of eliciting the smallest pieces of factual information and displaying them as dispassionately as possible. It needs a Toynbee to set its development as one part of the whole sweeping progress of man's achievement and to place in a meaningful relationship to other activities. It needs academic historians who will write primarily for other historical bibliographers and so help to shape the course of future studies. It needs its competent popularizers who, basing their work on the best of modern scholarship, can interpret it to a general public. Also, in these days of the advances of local studies, it needs work to be done in understanding and interpreting the whole of the book trade in depth at a local level.

If any analogy with historical studies may, to some, appear somewhat fanciful, it is drawn deliberately to emphasize a relationship which is of paramount importance. Either historical bibliography is a part of the main or its development is certain to be severely restricted.

[1] *ALTICK*, R. D. *The English Common Reader. A social history of the mass reading public 1800–1900.* 1957.

Index

171